Facts ...and folklore

An Historical Guide to

Landmarks, Events, Activities, Parks, Beaches, Plants & Wildlife, Accommodations, Restaurants, Shops & Services

Salt Spring Island

By V.A. Lindholm

Hidden Lighthouse Publishers
Canadian Rockies/Vancouver/Victoria

Publication Information

Hidden Lighthouse Publishers
A division of Diskover Office Software Ltd.
575 Fernhill Rd
Site 3, Comp. 4
Mayne Island, BC V0N 2J0

© 2005-2006 Hidden Lighthouse Publishers

Extreme care has been taken to ensure that all information presented in this book is accurate and up-to-date, and neither the author nor the publisher can be held responsible for any errors.

Cover design, page design and composition by Vicky Lindholm
All photos, with the exception of those listed under Credits, by Vicky Lindholm
Maps by Vicky Lindholm

Front cover photo:
   A sunset, Salt Spring Island
Back cover photo:
   Long Harbour, Salt Spring Island

To Kevin Oke Photography
whose generous submission of photos
enabled me to complete this book on
time

Contents

Contents

Contents

A Tale of Salt Spring

Vesuvius Bay Wharf

It was in the spring of 1861 that a Scotsman, named Jonathan Begg, was awakened by a band of Haida Indians who were stealing from his store...

With Jonathan aboard, the British Royal Navy pursued the Indians in a gunboat named the H.M.G. *Forward*. When they found the Indians camped on Vancouver Island, they fired on their camp. In the exchange of gunfire, four Indians and one crewman were killed.[1]

Jonathan Begg was born in Scotland, in the early 1800's. In 1859, he arrived penniless, in what was at that time the Colony of Vancouver Island.[2]

Jonathan was among the first settlers to reform the land pre-emption system for the colony.[3] He then settled in that colony, on Salt Spring Island. There, he became **the Postman**, operating the Island's first store and post office.[4]

The politically minded Jonathan Begg was a reporter of the news, having been Salt Spring's correspondent for the *British Colonist* newspaper.[5] In response to his request for a post office, another newspaper said this about him:

From Mr. J. Begg, one of the first, and most respectable of the settlers on Salt Spring Island, we are rejoiced to hear a most satisfactory account of the prospects of their happy little community.

New Westminster Times[6]

Salt Spring Island

THiNgS to KNoW

Just sit right back and you'll hear a tale...

Salt Spring is a bustling island in the southern Gulf Islands. It lies in the rain shadow of the Vancouver Island Mountains, which protects it from storms that blow in from the Pacific Ocean. Often referred to as the *Banana Belt* of Canada, the Islands have a Mediterranean-type climate, which is warm during the day and cool at night.

Salt Spring Island enjoys an average of 2,000 hours of sunshine, annually. With the longest frost-free season in the country, spring begins as early as February. Because it rarely snows, a winter weekend on Salt Spring can be quite cozy with some logs on a *paia* (fire).

At 180 sq km, Salt Spring is the largest of the southern Gulf Islands. Its rolling hills and roads are reminiscent of an English *Illahee* (countryside). There are few traffic lights, curbs and sidewalks, making it quite a quaint attraction.

Although most of the Gulf Islands are uninhabited, Salt Spring is the fastest growing and most populous of the southern Gulf Islands.

At the time of this writing, the Island had a population of about 10,000 permanent residents, of which most are young families, retirees and business professionals.

Known as *The Art Lover's Gallery*, Salt Spring is home to the greatest collection of artists in all of Canada. During the tourist season, the population swells to around 20,000.

Part-time residents own cottages as their 'home away from home', living as *weekenders* (people who spend weekends on Salt Spring) during the tourist season.

Salt Spring Island

Ganges

Urbanization of the Island began at its north end, when a group of settlers arrived during the gold rush in the late 1850's. Most of these immigrants were Black men, who were former slaves from the United States. They were followed immediately by Australians and settlers of other descents.[7]

Soon, a community called *Central Settlement* developed in an inner location at the north end. Of the 26 families that settled there, 17 were Black.[8]

The settlers found the winter of 1862 to be unusually severe, which resulted in a 30 percent decrease in the Island's population.[9]

Then, after the Civil War, many of the Black residents returned to the U.S.[10]

However, as more women and children arrived in the 1870's[11] communities began to develop in each of the corners of the Island.[12]

Some of the families who settled at the south end were *Kanakas* (people of Hawaiian descent).[13] By that time, the Island's population had tripled[14] and it held claim to being the first agricultural settlement in all of British Columbia.[15]

Over the next decade, British and Irish immigrants began to settle on the Island[16] and, soon, another community began to develop, near a harbour called *Ganges Harbour*. The community became known as *Ganges*.[17]

Main street through Ganges in 1948 – Salt Spring Archives CKC998162076

Salt Spring Island

Today, Ganges is 'downtown' to Salt Spring Islanders. As the commercial hub of Salt Spring, it is the largest community in all the Gulf Islands.

Ganges provides for grocery stores, restaurants, banks, art galleries, retail stores and other businesses, as well as a marina. A visitor information centre is located in the heart of the village.

Ganges main street as it appears today

Vesuvius Bay Wharf

In the 1860's, ships traveling to Vancouver Island sailed past both the east and west sides of Salt Spring. Passengers were landed by boat, off *Trincomali Channel*, on the northeast side of the Island, or in *Vesuvius Bay* on the northwest side of the Island.[18]

Vesuvius Bay wharf at the turn of the century – Salt Spring Archives 50532

The first wharf was built in Vesuvius Bay in the 1870's.[19] It accommodated ships coming through the waterway called *Stuart Channel*.

By the 1890's, five wharves had been constructed on the Island. A wharf in **the Postman's** community of *Fernwood* serviced the northern tip of the Island.[20]

Wharves in *Vesuvius Bay* and *Ganges Harbour* serviced the communities on the northwest and northeast sides, while wharves in *Fulford Harbour* and *Burgoyne Bay* serviced the southeast and southwest sides.[21]

Wharf in Ganges Harbour in 1907
Salt Spring Archives 1994137002

At the onset of World War I, a new 300 m wharf was constructed in Ganges Harbour to provide deepwater docking on any tide.[22] By the 1930's, it had replaced the wharf in Vesuvius Bay as the main port of call.[23]

S.S. *Princess Elaine* at Ganges wharf in 1928
Salt Spring Archives CKC998162123

Today, there are three main wharves on Salt Spring. The newest wharf is located at *Long Harbour*, north of Ganges Harbour. Acquired in the 1960's, it services large ferries traveling to and from the mainland.[24]

The wharf in Fulford Harbour provides for the most demanding ferry terminal on the Island, servicing ferries traveling to and from the tip of Vancouver Island.

The Vesuvius Bay wharf still serves as a port of call, but for smaller ferries traveling to and from the east side of Vancouver Island.

Ganges Post Offices

In the late 1850's, **the Postman** began offering a postal service from the store he owned in Fernwood.[25] A schooner would pass by his property three times a week[26] and he would row out into the Channel to collect the mail from one of the crew.[27]

The store was initially named the *Salt Spring Island Store*, but was later renamed the *Balmoral Store*.[28] Although it soon became a gathering place for the families living in Fernwood,[29] **the Postman** sold the business three years after it opened[30] and the post office closed.

Later, in the 1870's, the *Salt Spring Island Post Office* opened in a little, one-room shack in Central Settlement. An obstinate mule delivered the mail. Whenever the mule decided to run past a mail delivery point, its rider would drop a note apologizing for not delivering the mail that day.[31]

Around that same time, a Portuguese storekeeper opened a second post office, from his store in Vesuvius. He would sail to Vancouver Island to purchase goods for his store. At one time, it was the only store on the Island.[32]

Vesuvius Post Office in the 1950's
Salt Spring Archives 02186028

The post office in Vesuvius closed shortly after it opened.[33] Much later, in the 1970`s, the 100-year old building was destroyed by fire.[34] Today, the *Vesuvius Inn Neighborhood Pub* sits on the site.

Site of the Vesuvius Post Office
as it appears today

In the 1890's, a settler opened another store on the Island, from his home in Central. Then, he took over the Salt Spring Island Post Office and moved it into his store.[35]

Salt Spring Island Post Office, 1890's
Salt Spring Archives 2005009001

The settler called his store *Broadwell`s Store*. It was the largest store on the Island.[36] In the 1930`s, the Salt Spring Island Post Office closed.[37] Today, a fire hall sits on the site.

Site of the Salt Spring Island Post Office as it appears today

At the turn of the century, another post office opened, near the Ganges wharf.[38] It operated from a building that was attached to the back of a boarding house.[39]

Ganges Post Office in the 1930's Salt Spring Archives 1994137010

The S.S. *Iroquois* would deliver the mail to the Ganges wharf, at which time the ship's purser would often open up the ship's bar to the settlers who were waiting for their mail.[40]

Much later, in the 1950's, the boarding house in Ganges was demolished, along with the attachment that had served as the post office.[41] Today, a toy store, called *West of the Moon*, sits on the site and two post offices in Ganges serve the north end.

Fulford Post Office

Between 1880 and 1893, three post offices opened at the south end.[42] At the turn of the century, two of them were moved into a valley, called the *Fulford-Burgoyne Valley*.[43]

When they were moved, they were consolidated as one post office, called the *South Salt Spring Island Post Office*.[44] It served the two communities there.

The consolidated post office operated from a store called *R.P. Edwards' Store*. The storekeeper was known locally as 'Old Edwards'. He would wait until he heard the ship's whistle before loading the mail bags into his cart. The ship's Captain would then wait impatiently as he wheeled the cart down the long road to the Fulford Harbour wharf.[45]

During its final voyage of 1911, the S.S. *Iroquois* was delivering the mail to the post office. After it sank, a mailbag that was on board washed ashore. One of the letters it contained was addressed to a settler who lived in the valley. It was from the government, appointing him Justice of the Peace.[46]

At the end of World War I, the post office was moved into a hotel overlooking the harbour. It was called the *White Lodge*.[47]

Fulford Post Office in 1920
Salt Spring Archives 1994137040

In the 1920's, another post office opened, at a small south end community called *Musgrave Landing*.[48] Once again, there were three post offices serving the south end; one at Fulford Harbour, a second at Musgrave Landing and a third at a community called *Beaver Point*.[49]

Beaver Point Post Office in the 1920's
Salt Spring Archives 1994137036

Shortly thereafter, the post office at Fulford Harbour was renamed the *Fulford Harbour Post Office*.[50] In the 1930's, the hotel from which it operated was destroyed by fire and rebuilt. Today, the *Fulford Inn* sits on the site.

A decade later, the post office was moved into a store at the wharf. In the early 1950's, the building was converted into a concession, called *Mary Lee's Snack Shop*. Four years later, new owners changed the name to *Nan's Coffee Bar*.[51]

**Fulford Post Office in the late 1950's
Salt Spring Archives 02186003**

Around that time, the other post offices at the south end closed, leaving only the Fulford Harbour Post Office in operation.[52] Today, the building that

housed the post office is home to the *Tree House Café South* and the post office operates from around the corner.

Salt Spring Elementary School

In the early 1860's, a log schoolhouse was built in Central. It was called the *Vesuvius School*. A few years later, it was destroyed and a similar log building was built on the same site to replace it.[53]

**Vesuvius School in the 1860's
Salt Spring Archives 1994137167**

The first teacher to teach at the school was Black. Each week, he would teach three days at the schoolhouse, and then walk to the property of **the Postman**, where he would teach three days in an abandoned log cabin. For several years, he received no payment for his instruction.[54]

By the 1880's, a frame building had been constructed near the log schoolhouse and the school was moved there. At that time, the log schoolhouse became a location for community meetings and church services.[55]

By the turn of the century, there were five public schools on Salt Spring;[56] three at the north end and two at the south end. Over the next two decades, two more public schools opened.[57]

Unfortunately, by the year 1940, the depression of the previous decade had forced the Island to amalgamate most of its schools into one building, in Ganges. Named the *Consolidated School*, it provided for grades 1-12.[58]

Salt Spring Elementary School in 1940 - Salt Spring Archives 0001

When the Consolidated School opened, only two other schools remained in operation. In the 1950's, those schools also closed.[59]

By the 1960's, the Consolidated School had been renamed the *Salt Spring Elementary School*.[60]

Salt Spring Island

Salt Spring Elementary School as it appears today

The Chicken House School, early 1900's Salt Spring Archives CKC998162047

Today, there are five elementary schools on the Island. The Salt Spring Elementary School is located in Ganges, on Rainbow Road.

Gulf Islands Secondary School

Until the end of World War I, Salt Spring students could only attain grade eight. However, in the early 1920's, classes began for grades 9 and 10 in a former police building.[61]

A few years later, the Salt Spring Island Farmers Institute offered the school a more suitable building, which had been used to house poultry during the fall fair. The school was named the *Ganges High School*, but was jokingly referred to as the *Chicken House School*.[62]

The first year, 23 students in grades 9 and 10 attended the school. The students paid a monthly fee to attend and were responsible for their own books and transportation.[63]

In the 1960's, a new high school was built, on a hill beside the elementary school. It was called the *Gulf Islands Secondary School*.[64]

Recently, the high school was moved into a new building on Rainbow Road. The *Scholar Ship* (a water taxi that carries school children) transports children to the high school, from neighboring Islands.

Mary HaWkiNS MeMorial Library

Just before the turn of the century, the first library opened in the store in Central. The library consisted of 60 books.[65]

Later, in the early 1930's, an actress opened a pay lending library above a store in Ganges. In the 1950's, 12 women established a library as a centennial project, in a back room of the store.[66] It was named the *Centennial Library* and it opened with 1,300 donated books.[67]

Within a decade, the library had acquired more than 5,000 books. When it was decided that a larger building was required, a boat-building workshop was purchased and the library was moved there the following year.[68]

Several years later, the library, which had doubled in size, purchased a small house on an adjacent property. The staff enlarged the library by attaching it to the house. At that time, it was the only library in all of British Columbia that contained a bathtub.[69]

In the 1970's, the library was renamed the *Mary Hawkins Memorial Library.*[70] At last count, it maintained a collection of at least 43,000 books.

Today, about 150 volunteers staff the library, making it the largest all-volunteer library in Canada. The library is located in Ganges, on McPhillips Avenue. The bathtub has been removed.

Mouat's Mall

At the turn of the century, two settlers went into partnership and purchased the store in Central. Then, they constructed a large building in Ganges and moved the store there.[71]

Their new store included a blacksmith shop and some sheds, which sat near the Ganges wharf. Using two boats, the partners operated a large export business from their store.[72]

When one of the partners died three years later, a widow and one of her sons purchased the business. They sold everything from groceries and shoe polish to tools and furniture.[73] They also operated the post office in Ganges.

Initially, the widow and her son named the store *G.J. Mouat and Company*.[74] When her oldest son joined the business later, it was renamed *Mouat Brothers Company Ltd.*[75]

By then, the wharf had become known as *Mouat's Landing*. Customers would gather there to socialize on *boat days* (when boats would dock at the wharf). They would leave their saddle ponies,

ox teams, buggies and wagons all around the wharf.[76]

Just before the outbreak of World War I, a new building was constructed next door and the store was moved there.[77]

The new store had a wide staircase and a long counter that spanned the length of the store. The staircase led to a landing, and then split into two sets of stairs that continued up to the second floor.[78]

Mouat's Mall in the 1920's - Salt Spring Archives CKC998162061

There was a large feed shed at Mouat's Landing, with a separate room for kerosene, naphtha gas and lubricating oil. The shed had an office inside, with a stand up desk on which sat a telephone that was connected to the store.[79]

In the late 1960's, the company assets were purchased by a group of individuals that included the widow's grandsons. At that time, a new company was formed and the store was renamed *Mouat's Trading Company Ltd.*[80]

Salt Spring Island

Over time, the feed shed was connected to the store to form a building complex. It was called *Mouat's Mall*.

> **Treasure Hunt**
> *There is a mural of an Arbutus tree on the side of a building. Can you find it in Ganges?*

Today, the store provides for hardware and housewares and the mall is leased to businesses that are known collectively as *Seaside at Mouat's*. At the time of this writing, the businesses in Mouat's Mall included a salon, a bookstore, a gallery and a restaurant.

Mouat's Trading Company celebrates its centennial in the year 2007. The mall is located in Ganges, at the end of Fulford-Ganges Road.

Mouat's Mall as it appears today

Salt Spring Island

Grace Point Square

Grace Point Square is a building complex that offers a variety of shops, restaurants, galleries and other businesses. It is located in Ganges, at the end of Fulford-Ganges Road.

Creekhouse & Creekside

Built across a creek in Ganges, which flows between Fulford-Ganges Road and McPhillips Avenue, Creekhouse & Creekside are building complexes that house local businesses.

At the time of this writing, the buildings provided for a breakfast café, photographic studio, video store, and numerous shops and services.

> **Treasure Hunt**
> *A school of fish swims along a fence. Can you find them on Salt Spring?*

Salt Spring Island Trading Company

In the 1890's, a wealthy, but generous, Englishman immigrated to Salt Spring. He was always formally dressed, with a satin top hat and a long black frock. He liked to be called 'the Squire'.[81]

Just before the outbreak of World War I, the English Squire and some other settlers built a general store in Ganges, called the *Salt Spring Island Trading Company*.[82]

Soon, the Squire's store became a direct competitor of the Mouat brothers' store. Nevertheless, the relationship between the store owners remained friendly.[83]

Salt Spring Island

Salt Spring Island Trading Company in the 1930's - Salt Spring Archives 02186020

The store operated until the late 1960`s, when it was bought out by the Mouat brothers.[84] At that time, it was renamed the *Gulf Islands Trading Co. Ltd.*[85]

Over time, additional businesses were established alongside the store. Today, the building complex is, once again, called the Salt Spring Island Trading Company.

At the time of this writing, the businesses included a long-lived shoe store, as well as a health food store, a fitness center, a bookstore and a café. The building complex is located in Ganges, on Lower Ganges Road.

Salt Spring Island Trading Company as it appears today

Salt Spring Island

Ganges Village Market Centre

The *Ganges Village Market Centre* is a busy mall in Ganges. At the time of this writing, the businesses in the mall included a pizza parlor, fitness center, pharmacy, video store and department store.

The mall, which is located on Lower Ganges Road, also provides for a supermarket and post office.

Salt Spring Island Fire Department

In the 1940's, a Salt Spring Islander used a welding torch to add a tank and a pump to an old black Buick. The Buick was then painted bright red and it became Salt Spring's first fire truck. The fire chief used an old motor horn as a siren.[86]

At that time, the Salt Spring Island Trading Company looked out over the ocean.[87] In the early 1960's, a landfill was created in front of it and a fire hall was built on the site.[88]

A few years later, the Island hired its first *high muckymuck* (fire chief)[89] and a volunteer fire brigade was formed.

Today, the *Salt Spring Island Fire Department* provides for eight fire trucks, one emergency vehicle, four *smoke eaters* (fire fighters) and 31 volunteers. It is located in the heart of Ganges.

RCMP Station

In the 1860's, one of the first settlers to arrive on Salt Spring turned in his wife for poisoning a neighbor. Six years later, he became the constable for the Island. His equipment consisted of a musket, handcuffs and a canoe.[90]

In the 1880's, the first *gaol* (jail) to exist in the southern Gulf Islands was built in Central.[91] It was a small, square, white jailhouse that contained just two cells.[92] There were wooden bars on the windows and a padlock on the door.[93]

Throughout the following decade, although a single constable was responsible for law enforcement on Salt Spring, the two jail cells were only used five times.[94]

Today, there are over 6,000 *Queen's Cowboys* (RCMP) employed in British Columbia. However, on Salt Spring, one sergeant, two corporals and five constables provide law enforcement on the Island. The RCMP station is located in Ganges, on Lower Ganges Road.

Lady Minto Hospital

At the start of World War I, a retired British army doctor donated some land for a hospital near Ganges. The hospital was first named the *Gulf Islands (Cottage) Hospital,*[95] but was later renamed the *Lady Minto Gulf Islands Hospital.*[96]

Initially, the hospital had two wards, each of which contained three beds. The year following its construction, a third ward was added.[97]

A small shed that was used as the Morgue stood behind the hospital. The medical staff would prepare the dead, put them on a stretcher and carry them down a dark path to the Morgue.[98]

Old Lady Minto Hospital in the 1930's
Salt Spring Archives 02186014

In the 1930's, a nurse's residence opened and the facility grew to become an 18-bed hospital. A decade later, an x-ray machine and sterilizer were installed.[99] Unfortunately, the sterilizer was so old that every time they used it, the staff was afraid it would explode.[100]

For 40 years, the Lady Minto Hospital was the only hospital in all the Gulf Islands. Then, in the 1950's, it was replaced with a larger building that was built nearby.[101]

For a while thereafter, the old hospital building served as a dormitory for schoolchildren from the other Gulf Islands who attended the secondary school in Ganges.[102] In the 1970's, it was taken over by the Salt Spring Island Community Society.[103] It now operates as a community center.

At the time of this writing, the new hospital provided for 10 general practitioners and five specialists, two ambulances and 32 volunteer paramedics.

Gulf Islands Veterinary Clinic

Salt Spring has more pets than it has people. It offers numerous grooming services, hospitals, boarding facilities and supply stores for its pets. There is even a Salt Spring branch of the SPCA.

Old Lady Minto Hospital as it appears today

Today, the new Lady Minto Hospital is located on Crofton Road. It offers 50 beds, as well as emergency, operating and maternity rooms, and full laboratory, ultrasound and x-ray facilities.

Salt Spring Island

The *Gulf Islands Veterinary Clinic* is operated by a farm veterinarian. The clinic, which is located in Ganges, on Lower Ganges Road, provides for full service surgery, dentistry, medicine, laboratory and x-ray facilities.

Thrifty Foods

In the late 1960's, the area behind the fire hall was still a tidal inlet that contained log booms.[104]

Site of Thrifty Foods in the 1960's - Salt Spring Archives CKC998162110

In the year 1970, the site was filled in to provide more parking and retail space for Mouat's Store.[105] Soon, a grocery store opened in part of the space.

Today, *Thrifty Foods* is one of the busiest grocery stores in all of Canada. The supermarket carries fresh baking, produce and dairy products, as well as meats. It is located in Ganges, at Mouat's Landing.

Salt Spring Island

Places to Stay

Just before the outbreak of World War I, a hotel was erected in Ganges, beside what would later become the Salt Spring Island Trading Company. The hotel was called the *Ganges Hotel* and, at that time, it was the largest building on Salt Spring.[106]

The hotel had 30 guest rooms, each with hot and cold water. Four rooms had private baths. Rooms cost upwards of $2.50 per night, including meals.[107]

Ganges Hotel in 1912 - Salt Spring Archives 50580

Ganges Hotel on fire in 1913
Salt Spring Archives 50481

Unfortunately, in its very first year of operation, the magnificent Ganges Hotel was destroyed by fire.

Today, you can see some good examples of turn-of-the-century architecture around Salt Spring. Some of the Inns and lodges are still in operation. However, although there are numerous accommodations on the Island, only a small selection have been listed in this little book.

Balmoral By The Sea B&B

The *Balmoral by the Sea B&B* is a bed and breakfast at the north end. It is located on the shores of Long Harbour, on Scott Point Drive. Phone: 1-800-905-5117

Angel Cottage

Angel Cottage is a charming, pet-friendly cottage rental at the north end. It is located near Fernwood, on North End Road. Phone: (250) 537-8350

BeachHouse B&B

The *BeachHouse B&B* is a pet-friendly bed and breakfast at the south end. It is located at Fulford Harbour, on Isabella Point Road. Phone: 1-888-653-6334

Tir Aluinn

Tir Aluinn is a cottage rental at the north end. It is located near Fernwood, on West Eagle Drive. Phone: (250) 537-9387

Anchor Point Bed & Breakfast

The *Anchor Point Bed and Breakfast* is a B&B at the north end. It is located on the shores of Ganges Harbour, on Beddis Road. Phone: 1-800-648-2560

Vesuvius Beach B&B

The *Vesuvius Beach B&B* is a bed and breakfast at the north end. It is located in Vesuvius, on Bayview Road. Phone: (250) 537-4123

Salt Spring Island Hostel

Salt Spring Island Hostel provides for a dormitory-style accommodation at the north end. Guests have the use of a common kitchen and living area. It is located at Cusheon Lake, on Cusheon Lake Road. Phone: (250) 537-4149

Booth Bay B&B

Just before the onset of World War I, a boat builder purchased some property on a bay. There, he began construction of a large, waterfront, frame house.[108]

The following year, the boat builder sold his property. The new owner completed the house, adding upswept ends that gave the building a unique characteristic.[109]

In the 1940's, the property was sold to a couple who converted it into a resort, called *Aclands*. Several years later, new owners built some guest cottages on the property and changed the name of the resort to the *Booth Bay Resort*.[110]

Later, in the 1970's, the property was sold yet again and a restaurant, called *The Bay Window*, was opened on the property.[111] The resort ceased to operate in the 1990's.[112]

Today, the home is operated as the *Booth Bay Bed and Breakfast*. The B&B is located at the north end, near Vesuvius, on Acland Road. Phone: (250) 538-5544

CRaNBerry Ridge Bed & BreaKFast

The *Cranberry Ridge Bed and Breakfast* is a B&B at the north end. It is located near Ganges, on Don Ore Road. Phone: 1-888-537-4854

HarBouR HouSe HoteL

In the 1890's, a settler emigrated from Ireland to Salt Spring. Initially, he worked on a farm overlooking Ganges Harbour. A decade later, he purchased the farm and renamed it *Harbour House.*[113]

While the settler was serving in World War I, his wife and brother-in-law converted the farmhouse into a guesthouse, adding several bedrooms and a dining room. They also set up some tents on the property.[114] They called their guesthouse the *Harbour House Hotel.*

The hotel became a popular destination and, soon, they expanded it and added a tennis court.[115] In the 1920's, they added two additional tennis courts, a beer parlor and a glassed-in dance pavilion, called the 'Sun Room'. There was also a drawing room and a lounge, in which they kept roaring fires.[116]

The guests participated in crab races on the billiard table, bridge, beachfront swimming and scavenger hunts. The hotel dances attracted as many as 100 people.[117]

In the 1940's, the tents on the grounds were replaced with cabins[118] and by the 1960's, a swimming pool had replaced one of the three tennis courts.[119]

A decade later, the hotel was destroyed by fire[120] and rebuilt. Today, it offers 35 rooms and facilities for small conferences, weddings and other special events. The hotel is located at the north end, in Ganges, on Upper Ganges Road. Phone: 1-888-799-5571

Salt Spring Island

Sky Valley Inn B&B

The *Sky Valley Inn B&B* is a bed and breakfast at the north end. It is located near Cusheon Lake, on Sky Valley Road. Phone: (250) 537-9800

Monivea Bed & Breakfast

The *Monivea Bed and Breakfast* is a pet-friendly B&B at the north end. It is located near Ganges, on Fulford-Ganges Road. Phone: (250) 537-5856

Ganges Hill B&B

The *Ganges Hill B&B* is a bed and breakfast at the north end. It is located in Ganges, on Fulford-Ganges Road. Phone: (250) 537-5856

Salt Springs Spa Resort

Salt Springs Spa Resort accesses one of 14 salt springs at the north end. The spa provides guests with therapeutic mineral baths. The resort and spa are located on the eastern shore, in Fernwood, on North Beach Road. Phone: 1-800-665-0039

Mountain Aerie Bed & Breakfast

The *Mountain Aerie Bed and Breakfast* is a B&B at the north end. It is located near Ganges, on Wilkie Way. Phone: 1-878-501-5005

Casa del Mar

Casa del Mar is a cottage rental at the north end. It is located near Fernwood, on North End Road. Phone: (250) 537-5326

The Old Farmhouse Bed & Breakfast

In the 1890`s, a British dairyman settled with his family on Salt Spring. A few years later, he purchased some property at the north end, where he built a farmhouse.[121] Over time, an Arbutus tree could be seen growing near the house.

Old Farmhouse B&B, early 1900's
Management of Old Farmhouse B&B

One hundred years later, new owners converted the property into a bed and breakfast. Today, it is operated as the *Old Farmhouse B&B*. The Arbutus in the yard is now the largest on the Island.

Salt Spring Island

The bed and breakfast is adult-oriented and pet-friendly. There are also facilities for weddings. It is located at the north end, near Ganges, on North End Road. Phone: (250) 537-4113

Old Farmhouse B&B as it appears today

Cloud 9 Oceanview B&B

The *Cloud 9 Oceanview B&B* is a 4½ star bed and breakfast at the north end. It is located on the eastern shore, near Fernwood, on Sun Eagle Drive. Phone: 1-877-722-8233

Arbutus Point Oceanfront B&B

The *Arbutus Point Oceanfront B&B* is a pet-friendly bed and breakfast at the north end. It is located on the shores of Long Harbour, on Welbury Drive. Phone: 1-888-633-9555

Hastings House Country Estate

In the mid-1800's, the Hudson's Bay Company established a fortified trading post [122] at Ganges Harbour. The trading post was the first structure ever built on Salt Spring.

Much later, in the 1930's, a naval architect immigrated to Canada, from England. Shortly thereafter, he purchased the waterfront property overlooking the harbour.

When he began to establish a farm on the property, the architect moved the trading post inland [123] and built a Sussex-style Manor House on the site. In his home, he worked on secret designs for the British Royal Navy. [124]

Salt Spring Island

Today, the property operates as a world-renowned luxury Inn, called the *Hasting's House Country Estate Hotel*. The Inn, which has won numerous awards, offers 18 guest suites in seven restored buildings at the north end.

The Tudor-style home and farmhouse each provide for two suites. The original Hudson's Bay trading post serves as a two-room cottage, called 'The Post'. The original barn contains additional suites and a spa.

The Inn and spa are located on the shores of Ganges Harbour, on Upper Ganges Road. At the time of this writing, the Inn was celebrating its centennial. Phone: 1-800-661-9255

Paradise Hills Guesthouse

The *Paradise Hills Guesthouse* is a cottage rental at the north end. It is located near Fernwood, on Stark's Road. Phone: 1-800-242-9570

Fulford Creek Guest House

At the turn of the century, a settler established a farm for his family in the Fulford-Burgoyne Valley. Initially, a small cabin was their homestead.[125]

Salt Spring Island

When the family outgrew the cabin in the 1920's, they built a four-bedroom farmhouse nearby. During the 1940's, the house was used as a boarding house for migrant farm workers. A decade later, it became a nursing home.[126]

Today, the farmhouse operates as the *Fulford Creek Guest House*. The pet-friendly cottage rental is located at the south end, near Fulford Harbour, on Fulford-Ganges Road. Phone: 1-866-697-4949

Pond House on Salt Spring

The *Pond House on Salt Spring* is a cottage rental at the north end. It is located at Long Harbour, on Long Harbour Road. Phone: 1-888-760-8148

Salt Spring Cottages

In the 1860's, the Portuguese settler who would later own the store and post office in Vesuvius immigrated to Salt Spring.[127]

Around the 1880's, the settler constructed three houses on Vesuvius Bay. The houses were built as dowries for three of his six daughters. However, because the vacant homes were built to be lived in after his daughters were wed, they were often rented out.[128]

Eventually, the houses were sold and remodeled. One of the homes was moved up a hill[129] where it overlooked the bay.

Dowry houses on Vesuvius Beach in the 1890's - Salt Spring Archives 093a

Today, the house on the hill is a pet-friendly cottage rental, operated by *Salt Spring Cottages*. The cottage still looks out over the bay. It is located at the north end, in Vesuvius, on Langley Road. Phone: 1-877-537-1903

The Dowry house as it appears today

Fulford Inn

By the 1890's, a tavern, called *Roger's Saloon*, had opened at the head of Fulford Harbour. At the turn of the century, it was destroyed by fire[130] and the property was sold.

One day, the new owner heard a rumor that the highways crew were planning to build a road over the bank across the nearby creek. Its construction would cut off the corner on which his property sat.[131]

The owner of the property knew that a bylaw existed, which prohibited the destruction of a fruit orchard during the construction of a highway. So he promptly planted fruit trees all over his newly acquired property. Subsequently, a bend in the road from Fulford to Ganges was created at the head of the harbour.[132]

Salt Spring Island

A few years later, the property changed hands again. The new owner, who was known locally as 'Pop', erected a store on the property. [133]

Soon, he expanded the store and opened a hotel. Initially, the hotel was called the *White House Hotel*, but was later renamed the *White Lodge*. [134] During the 1920's, it also served as the home of the post office at Fulford Harbour. [135]

The Fulford Inn in 1920 - Salt Spring Archives 1994137041

The hotel was destroyed by fire in the 1930's. When it was rebuilt, it was renamed the *Fulford Inn*. In the 1950's, it was again destroyed by fire and rebuilt. [136]

Today, the hotel, which was designed as a Tudor-style Inn, is one of the oldest Inns in all the Gulf Islands. The Inn is located at the south end, on the shores of Fulford Harbour, on Fulford-Ganges Road. Phone: 1-800-652-4432.

Fulford Inn as it appears today

Salt Spring Island

Cusheon Lake Resort

Cusheon Lake Resort provides for 14 log cabins and two cedar chalets at the north end. It is located on the shores of Cusheon Lake, on Natalie Lane. Phone: 1-866-899-0017

Spindrift at Welbury Point

Spindrift at Welbury Point is a pet-friendly cottage rental at the north end. It is located at Long Harbour, on Welbury Point Drive. Phone: (250) 537-5311

Ruckle Provincial Campground

Ruckle Provincial Campground is the largest provincial campground in all the Gulf Islands. The spectacular campground offers 70 walk-in waterfront sites. It is located at the south end, near Fulford, on Beaver Point Road.

Salt Spring Island Sights & Activities

1 The Movie Gallery
2 Island Star Video
3 The Wall
4 Kanaka Skate Park
5 Salt Spring Golf & Country Club
6 Hart Memorial Disc Golf Course
7 ArtSpring Theatre
8 Heritage House Museum
9 Portlock Recreational Park
10 Salt Spring Cinema
12 Salt Spring Center of Yoga
13 Blackburn Meadows Golf Course
14 Everlasting Summer
15 Akerman Museum
16 St. Paul`s Catholic Church

Things to See & Do

Salt Spring Island offers its visitors a variety of things to see and do. It provides for concerts, theatre productions, art shows and museums. Recreational activities include bowling, billiards, swimming, kayaking, sailing, fishing, golf, frisbee golf, skateboarding, tennis and climbing.

The Island consists of five major routes. Fulford-Ganges Road runs north and south, connecting Ganges to the Fulford ferry terminal. Upper Ganges Road, which turns into Vesuvius Bay Road connects Ganges to the Vesuvius ferry terminal. Long Harbour Road connects Ganges to the Long Harbour ferry terminal.

Lower Ganges Road turns into North End Road, which turns into Sunset Drive, circumventing the north end. Beaver Point Road connects the Fulford ferry terminal to the communities at the south end.

St. Paul's Catholic Church

In the year 1880, the construction of a Catholic church began on Salt Spring.[137] Much of its construction was performed by Hawaiians, who were later buried in the adjoining cemetery.[138] Thereafter, the church was the center of Hawaiian life for many years.[139]

The windows, door and bell for the church came from an Indian reserve on Vancouver Island. The materials were transported by canoe to Burgoyne Bay, and then by stoneboat to Fulford.[140]

St. Paul's Catholic Church and rectory at the turn of the century - Salt Spring Archives 083a

Eventually, the exterior siding and part of the interior were faced with imitation stone,[141] making it one of the most beautiful churches on Salt Spring.

St. Paul's Catholic Church as it appears today

Today, there are at least six historic churches that visitors to the Island can admire. Located in Fulford, on Fulford-Ganges Road, *St. Paul's Catholic Church* is the oldest church on the Island. (#16 on the map)

For a first-hand introduction to the heritage buildings in Ganges, you can contact Salt Spring Walking Tours. They provide one-hour strolls through the *rancherie* (village). Phone: (250) 537-1833

Heritage House Museum

In the 1870's, the Portuguese storekeepr constructed a grand home on Vesuvius Bay for his growing family. Soon, he converted his home and store into a hotel, called the *Vesuvius Bay Hotel*.[142]

In the 1880's, he built a little house to be used as overflow accommodations whenever there was no vacancy at his hotel. Unfortunately, one hundred years after its construction, the hotel was destroyed by fire.[143]

Fortunately, the little house survived. However, it soon became threatened by the expansion of the Vesuvius ferry terminal. So, in the year 1980, the Farmers Institute moved it to their grounds and a seniors group obtained a grant to convert it into a museum.[144]

Today, the four-room house is the home of the Island's first museum. Named the *Bittancourt Heritage House Museum*, it can be viewed by appointment. The museum is located in Ganges, on Rainbow Road. (#8 on the map) Phone: (250) 537-4895

Akerman Museum

In the early 1860's, an English settler purchased some land in the Fulford-Burgoyne Valley. There, he built a log home.[145]

Two year's later, he and his new wife built a larger, two-storey house beside a creek on their property. It was made from hand-hewn, squared timbers.[146]

In the 1880's, the couple converted part of their new house into the first store ever to operate in Fulford. Later, they converted it into the Island's first Inn and pub.[147] Called the *Traveler's Rest*, the Inn operated until the year 1910. The property was sold a decade later.[148]

One hundred years after the settler had acquired the property, his grandson purchased it.[149]

Throughout his life as road foreman, the settler's grandson had collected artifacts and craft pieces from Indian village life. After he had been living on the property a while, he built a museum beside the old Inn, in which to house his artifacts. He was over 80 years old at the time.[150]

Although the 140-year old Inn was recently demolished, the museum still operates on the property. It is located near Fulford, on Fulford-Ganges Road. (#15 on the map) It can be viewed by appointment. Phone: (250) 653-4228

Salt Spring Cinema

The very first hall to be built on Salt Spring was constructed in the 1890's, beside the school in Central. It was named the *Central Community Hall*.[151]

That year, the hall hosted the Island's first agricultural fair.[152] However, when it became apparent that the building was more suited to hosting indoor events, the fair was moved[153] and the hall went on to serve as a community center.

Salt Spring Island

Salt Spring Cinema in the 1930's - Salt Spring Archives 02186024

During the 1950's, events organizers would set up wooden folding chairs in the hall for special events. Then, a projectionist would display slides on a screen, while the local piano teacher played background music for the audience.[155]

In the 1970's, two wings, a stage and a porch were added to the hall.[156]

Today, the hall serves as a movie theatre, called *Salt Spring Cinema.* Located in Central, at the corner of North End and Vesuvius Bay Roads, it seats 120 people and offers a full concession stand.

A highlight of the cinema is the dynamic slide show that is shown before the feature film. (#10 on the map)

Salt Spring Cinema as it appears today

ArtSpring Theatre

In the late 1980's, a teacher, an actor and an architect began planning the creation of an arts centre on Salt Spring. When the centre was completed a decade later, it was called *ArtSpring*.[157]

Today, ArtSpring is a 265-seat performance and visual arts theatre. Open year-round, it is the Island's premier venue for concerts, theatre and exhibitions.

The presentations by many artists and performers at ArtSpring have a worldwide audience. The Salt Spring Singers, who have been making music for 30 years, put on concerts throughout the year. The Graffiti Theatre uses local talent to produce professional theatre. The Salt Spring Painters' Guild hosts various art exhibitions.

During its *Sizzling Summer Nights* music festival in July and August, ArtSpring hosts musical performances in all genres. The theatre is located in Ganges, on Jackson Avenue. (#7 on the map)

Hart Memorial Disc Golf Course

The *Hart Memorial Disc Golf Course* provides for frisbee golf. Once a popular camping location, the course now occupies an old camping oval in a beautiful old-growth forest.

The course is located in Ganges, in Mouat's Provincial Park on Seaview Avenue. The *Hart Memorial Disc Golf Tournament* takes place there each year. (#6 on the map)

Today, the farm is the home of the *Salt Spring Island Golf and Country Club*. The 9-hole course, which is open year-round, plays as a par 36. It features 10 tees and various teeing areas. One of the more challenging holes is a 454-yard, par 4 hole seven, which includes both a water hazard and a two-tiered green.

Salt Spring Golf & Country Club

In the 1890's, a Reverend took over a run-down farm in Central, where he lived in a log cabin on a dirt floor. Later, when his family arrived, a new home was built on the property. Eventually, the Reverend turned the property into a successful farm, called *Barnsbury Grange*.[158]

In the 1920's, the Reverend's son took over the property. He converted the farm into a golf course and the farmhouse into a clubhouse. Much later, in the 1960's, the clubhouse was destroyed by fire.[159]

Club cars and pull carts are available for rent. Facilities include a driving range and fully stocked pro shop. A new clubhouse also exists. The course is located in Ganges, on Lower Ganges Road. (#5 on the map)

Salt Spring Island

Blackburn Meadows Golf Course

The *Blackburn Meadows Golf Course* is a 9-hole links-style golf course and driving range located near Cusheon Lake, on Blackburn Road. As Canada's first organic golf course, the greens and fairways of the Blackburn Meadows course are maintained using only organic methods. (#13 on the map)

Salt Spring Centre of Yoga

Just after the turn of the century, a Scottish settler bought an acreage on Salt Spring.[160] Then, he hired a British builder to begin construction of a large, two-storey house. The plans for the house included a turret, a tower and a chapel.[161]

Unfortunately, just before the onset of World War I, the Scotsman ran out of money and abandoned the unfinished house. In the 1920's, he passed away, leaving his wife to rent it out.[162]

Eventually, the government took over the property. They renovated it, and then used it to run rehabilitation programs until after World War II.[163]

Later, in the early 1980's, the Dharma Sara Satsang Society converted the home into an holistic center. Today, the elegant house, which is known locally as the *Blackburn House*, is home to the *Salt Spring Centre of Yoga*.

Treasure Hunt
There is a mural of sea creatures painted on a buoy. Can you find it in a park?

The center offers programs that concentrate on body and spiritual awareness, and self-help techniques, such as yoga and tai chi. Located near Cusheon Lake, on Blackburn Road, the center is famous for its Swedan massage. (#12 on the map)

Kanaka Skate Park

The *Kanaka Skate Park* is a brand new skate park, with a small outdoor climbing wall. The park is located in Ganges, on Kanaka Road. (#4 on the map)

The Wall

The Wall is an indoor climbing facility. The facility, which is 7 m high, is located in Ganges, on Fulford-Ganges Road. (#3 on the map)

Everlasting Summer

At the turn of the century, a settler purchased some land in the Fulford-Burgoyne Valley. By the 1920's, the 81-year old man had become well known for his wonderful flower garden, which could be seen through an ivy-covered gate.[164]

The gardener tended his flower garden from morning until night. When visitors came for a tour, he would take them on a circular walk. He used a large, yet simple device, called a water-ram, to control the watering of his flowers.[165] It stood taller than his two-storey home.[166]

Much later, in the 1980's, a large flower, herb and rose garden, called *Everlasting Summer*, was established[167] near that same valley.

Today, the vast nursery produces over 200 plants and 75 varieties of roses. Thousands of flowers are then picked for drying.

Salt Spring Island

Dried flowers and floral arrangements can be purchased in a gift shop on the premises, which are located at the south end, on McLennan Drive. (#14 on the map)

Island Star Video

Island Star Video provides for movie rentals. It is located in Ganges, at Creekhouse. (#2 on the map) Alternatively, you can watch Salt Spring Cable on channel 12.

The Movie Gallery

The *Movie Gallery* provides for movie rentals. The store is located in Ganges, in the Ganges Village Market Centre. (#1 on the map)

Portlock Recreational Park

In the 1970`s, a recreational area was developed in Central. It was called *Portlock Recreational Park*.

Today, the park provides for a heated swimming pool, tennis courts, a soccer field, baseball diamonds, playgrounds and a .4 km track. It is located at the corner of North End and Vesuvius Bay Roads. (#9 on the map)

Places to Eat

The English Squire who started the Salt Spring Island Trading Company was a good cook and had a voracious appetite. He ate five meals a day with three helpings at dinner.[168]

The Squire would hire young orphaned boys to work on his estate property, and then teach them how to cook. While one boy worked in his mansion, the other would cook and serve his meals.[169]

At his dinner parties, he served seven-course meals at a very long table in his dining room. The meals would include soup and grapefruit, and large servings of halibut and roast beef. Dessert would consist of jellies and trifles, and lots of whipped cream.[170]

Today, there are numerous restaurants, bakeries and cafes on Salt Spring Island – too many to list in this little book. Many of the eateries offer food that is grown or raised on the Island.

Salt Spring is the organic growing capital of Canada. Of the 60 members of the Gulf Islands chapter of the society of Canadian Organic Growers, the majority operate on Salt Spring.

Many organic farmers employ *woofers* (willing workers on organic farms) as farm hands. Even the maintenance of one of its golf courses is organic.

The Morningside Organic Bakery and Café, in Fulford, is an organic delicatessen, bakery and coffee bar that offers organic bread, pastries and coffee. You can also get a slice of organic pizza there.

Whatever you hunger or thirst for, there are some terrific restaurants on Salt Spring Island where you can get great *muckamuck* (food) and drink. Keep in mind that roast leg of Salt Spring Lamb is considered a delicacy in gourmet restaurants throughout southwestern British Columbia.

For a first-hand introduction to the food that is available on the Island, you can contact Island Gourmet Safaris. They provide day-long, guided tours of the Island's finest food. Phone: (250) 537-4118

Moby's Marine Pub

Moby's Marine Pub is a licensed pub and restaurant that serves lunch and dinner, indoors or on their seaside patio. Live entertainment is provided. The pub is located in Ganges, on Upper Ganges Road. Phone: (250) 537-5559

Golden Island Restaurant

The *Golden Island Restaurant* offers Chinese cuisine for lunch and dinner. The restaurant is located in Ganges, in the Upper Ganges Centre on Lower Ganges Road. Phone: (250) 537-2535

Dagwood's Diner

Dagwood's Diner is a family restaurant that is open for breakfast, lunch and dinner. The diner is located in Ganges, in the Upper Ganges Centre on Lower Ganges Road. Phone: (250) 537-9323

Salt Spring Island

Fulford Inn

The *Fulford Inn* is a licensed pub and restaurant that serves lunch and dinner. A cold beer and wine store is also located on the premises. It has the largest, organic wine selection under one roof in all of British Columbia.

The pub provides for live music from some of the best performers in Canada. Musicians and singers, such as Randy Bachman, Valdy and Harry Manx, have all performed there. The restaurant and pub are located at Fulford Harbour, on Fulford-Ganges Road. Phone: 1-800-652-4432

The Tea Cozy

The *Tea Cozy* offers soups, sandwiches and pastries with a steaming cup of tea. The charming cafe specializes in home baking and loose leaf teas. It is located in Ganges, at Gasoline Alley on Fulford-Ganges Road.

House Piccolo

In the 1940's, the Dominion Government Telegraph and Telephone Company constructed a building to house a telephone exchange on Salt Spring.[171]

When the telephone company changed its system to dial telephones in the 1960's, the building became the home of an ice cream and candy store. Since then, it has operated as various restaurants.[172]

Today, the building is home to the *House Piccolo* restaurant, which features European and Scandinavian cuisine. Located in Ganges, on Hereford Avenue, the restaurant is open for dinner. Phone: (250) 537-1844

La Cucina Italian Grill

Open for breakfast, lunch and dinner, the *La Cucina Italian Grill* specializes in Italian-inspired cuisine with a West Coast twist. The restaurant is located in Ganges, at Mouat's Landing. Phone: (250) 537-5747

Hastings House Restaurant

The *Hasting's House Restaurant* provides for a formal dining room and superb wine cellar. It offers lunch and a five-course dinner menu that features West Coast cuisine. There is also a Sunday brunch.

The formal dining room is described as one of the top 10 in North American Inns. It is located in Ganges, on Upper Ganges Road. Reservations are recommended. Those who wish to dress in more casual attire can dine in 'The Snug', which is adjacent to the wine cellar. Phone: 1-800-661-9255

Shipstones English Pub

Shipstone's English Pub is an authentic British pub that is open for lunch and dinner, served indoors or on their seaside patio. The pub is located in Ganges, at Mouat's Landing. Live entertainment is provided. Phone: (250) 537-0700

Calvin□s Bistro

Calvin`s Bistro offers lunch and dinner, served indoors or on their seaside patio. They specialize in fresh seafood. The licensed bistro is located in Ganges, on Lower Ganges Road. Phone: (250) 538-5551

Oystercatcher Seafood Bar & Grill

The *Oystercatcher Seafood Bar and Grill* is open for lunch and dinner, served indoors or on their seaside patio. The restaurant is located in Ganges, at Mouat's Landing. Phone: (250) 537-5041

The Local

During World War I, prohibition closed all of the pubs on Salt Spring. So one settler started selling wine for 10 cents a jug. The settler would leave bottles of wine out on a stump and his customers would take what they wanted, and then leave their money[173] on the stump.

One day, the settler's dog barked at a customer who came to buy wine. After the customer complained, the police came to his home to investigate the incident. There, they discovered several 150 litre barrels of wine.[174]

The police arrested the settler and poured the wine into Ganges Harbour. Ironically, the judge imposed only a small fine on him, in an effort to preserve the Island's liquor supply.[175]

Later, in the early 1950's, 500 residents petitioned the Liquor Control Board for a liquor store. Because opposing residents submitted a counter-petition, it was several years later before Salt Spring acquired a liquor outlet.[176]

Today, a bar and bistro, called *The Local*, carries all the locally produced wines and beers, as well as a full supply of spirits. It is open for lunch and dinner, served indoors or on their seaside patio.

The bistro is located in Ganges, at Gasoline Alley on Fulford-Ganges Road. Live entertainment is provided.

Porter's Restaurant & Lounge

In the 1920's, the *Harbour House Hotel* acquired a cook who did not like customers gathering in his kitchen. When too many people came in at one time, he would throw pepper on his stove. The burning pepper would cause the customers to leave.[177]

Today, the hotel features a licensed pub and restaurant, called *Porter's Restaurant and Lounge*. Open for lunch and dinner, it provides for large meeting and banquet facilities. The restaurant is located in Ganges, on Upper Ganges Road. Phone: (250) 537-5571

Barbs Buns Bakery & Bistro

Barb's Buns Bakery & Bistro is a licensed restaurant that is open for breakfast and lunch. It offers vegetarian meals, soups and baked goods. Live, evening entertainment is provided on weekends.

On the fourth Thursday of each month, the bistro features an evening film festival, called The Film Festival Café, which has an evening menu. The bistro is located in Ganges, at Creekside. Phone: (250) 537-4491

AUNtie Pesto[]S Café & Deli

Auntie Pesto's Café & Deli is open for breakfast, lunch and dinner, served indoors or on their seaside patio. They feature espresso and desserts. The café is located at Ganges Harbour, in Grace Point Square. Phone: (250) 537-4181

EMbe Bakery

At the turn of the century, the brother of the Portuguese storekeeper constructed a stone building in Ganges, for use as a creamery.[178] Named the *Salt Spring Island Creamery*, it was a cooperative of dairy farmers.[179]

Initially, only farmers in the Ganges community sent their cream there. However, over time, other farmers starting supplying cream to the creamery. By the 1920's, the creamery was producing over 60,000 kg of butter.[180]

During that time, a truck driver would drive around the Island, picking up the cans of cream from all the farms along the road.[181]

When the ships would dock at the Ganges wharf, the driver would leave the empty cream cans and wait for the full ones to be unloaded from the ship. Some of the cans came from neighboring Galiano, Mayne and Pender Islands.[182]

One year, the creamery's butter was entered in the Canadian National Exhibition. It was awarded the distinction of being the best in all of Canada.[183]

Embe Bakery in the 1950's - Salt Spring Archives 02186016

The Salt Spring Island Creamery closed in the 1950's. After several additions were attached to the front of the building,[184] it became home to the *Embe Bakery*.

Treasure Hunt
A Fir tree that is 26' in diameter grows in Ruckle Park. Can you find it?

Today, the bakery offers soups, subs, breads, pastries and cakes. It is located in Ganges, on Fulford-Ganges Road.

Embe Bakery as it appears today

Artist's Bistro

The superb *Artist's Bistro* is located at Ganges Harbour, in Grace Point Square. The restaurant features West Coast cuisine. Phone: (250) 537-1701

Seaside Restaurant

The *Seaside Restaurant* in Vesuvius offers lunch and dinner, indoors or on their seaside patio. Located on Vesuvius Bay Road, they feature pasta, steak and seafood. Phone: (250) 537-2249

Raven Street Market Cafe

The *Raven Street Market Café* in Fernwood offers Canadian, wood-fired cuisine for lunch and dinner. The café is located on Fernwood Road. Phone: (250) 537-2273

The café is located in Ganges, at Mouat's Landing. Another location, called *Tree House Café South*, exists in Fulford. Phone: (250) 537-5379

Tree House Cafes

In the 1920's, a small building was built behind Mouat's Store. It housed an electric generator that powered the store. Later, it became a place where the butcher made sausage and prepared hams for smoking. [185]

Today, the building is home to an outdoor café, called the *Tree House Café North*. The café is open for breakfast, lunch and dinner. It also provides for live entertainment and features over 50 entertainers during 123 consecutive nights of music. On Thursday nights there is an open mike under a plum tree.

Places to Shop

In the year 1900, the brother of the Portuguese storekeeper opened his own store, in Ganges.[186] Four years later, he built a splendid house at the foot of Ganges Hill, and then moved his store there.[187]

Store in Ganges in 1920
Salt Spring Archives CKC998162131

Today, there are a variety of stores on Salt Spring Island where visitors can pick up a *potlatch* (gift) for *tillicum* (a friend). The Island offers numerous places to shop 'til you drop.

Salt Spring even has its own currency. Called 'Salt Spring Dollars', it is the very first alternative currency in Canada that is backed 100% by the Canadian dollar.

The currencies, which can be obtained at the Visitor Information Centre in Ganges, work like gift certificates and are accepted by most Salt Spring businesses. Each bill features the work of local artists.

Aroma Crystal Therapy

Aroma Crystal Therapy offers aromatherapy, jewelry, crystals, stones and healing gifts. The store is located in Ganges, at Gasoline Alley on Fulford-Ganges Road.

Mouat's Clothing Company

Mouat's Clothing Company offers two floors of casual Island wear for men and women, including clothing, footwear, accessories and athletic wear. The store is located in Ganges, at Mouat's Landing.

Salt Spring Island

The Housewares Store

The Housewares Store offers nearly 4,000 sq ft of space dedicated solely to quality housewares. The store is located in Ganges, at Mouat's Mall.

Side B Clothing Company

The *Side B Clothing Company* offers quality clothing for active men and women. It is located in Ganges, at Creekside.

Watermark Books

Watermark Books is a general bookstore that offers quality books. It is located in Ganges, on McPhillips Avenue.

Salt Spring Island

Old Salty Greetings, Gifts & Gourmet

Old Salty Greetings, Gifts and Gourmet offers a trendy collection of gifts and greeting cards for all ages. The store is located in Ganges, at Mouat's Landing.

Jambalaya

Jambalaya is a bead shop that also features a great selection of hats and scarves. The store is located in Fulford, on Fulford-Ganges Road.

Saltspring Soapworks

Saltspring Soapworks was started as a home-based business in a small cottage.[188] Today, the business operates in the heart of Ganges. It offers hand-made natural soaps using fragrances from the Gulf Islands. The store is located in Ganges, in the Harbour Market Building on Fulford-Ganges Road.

Solace Aromatherapy & Tea

Solace Aromatherapy and Tea offers quality aromatherapy products. The store is located in Fulford, on Morningside Drive.

Ganges Garment Company

The *Ganges Garment Company* specializes in quality clothing made in Canada. The store is located at Ganges Harbour, in Grace Point Square.

The Wardrobe

The Wardrobe is an eclectic clothing store that also offers hats and jewelry. The store is located in Fulford, on Morningside Drive.

Windflower Moon

Windflower Moon is a full range, metaphysical boutique that offers unique clothing and gift items produced by Island artists and other global locales. They also carry books on spiritual awareness, childbirth and mindful parenting. The store is located in Ganges, in the Harbour Market Building on Fulford-Ganges Road.

Salt Spring Island

Island Escapades

Island Escapade's offers quality athletic clothing and gear for the whole family. The store is located in Ganges, on Fulford-Ganges Road.

Houseboat

Houseboat offers housewares and accessories for West Coast home decor. The store is located in Ganges, on Hereford Avenue.

Stitches Quilts & Yarns

Initially, Methodist services at the north end took place in private homes, schools and community halls.[189]

At the turn of the century, the building of the *Vesuvius Bay Methodist Church* began in Central. The businesswoman who would later start Mouat's Store drove her horse and buggy across the Island to raise the necessary funds.[190]

In the 1920's, when several Protestant churches joined to form the United Church of Canada, the front portion of the church building was moved to Ganges and became the *Ganges United Church*.[191]

By the 1950's, the church had outgrown the structure. So they sold it to the Royal Canadian Legion,[192] who converted it into their hall.[193]

Stitches Quilts & Yarns as it appears today

Today, the front of the Vesuvius Bay Methodist Church is the home of *Stitches Quilts & Yarns*. Located in Ganges, on Hereford Avenue, it carries notions, fabric art supplies, embellishment kits, yarns and fabrics.

Stitches Quilts & Yarns in the 1960's
Salt Spring Archives L1

The structure served as the centre of Legion and Auxiliary activities until the 1980's.[194]

Flowers & Wine

Flowers & Wine offers wine, flowers and unique gifts. The charming store is located in Ganges, at Creekhouse.

Gypsy Island Tribal Boutique

The *Gypsy Island Tribal Boutique* offers trendy clothing and accessories. It is located in Ganges, on McPhillips Road.

Fables Cottage

Four years after the front portion of the Ganges United Church was moved to Ganges,[195] a manse was built for the Reverend and his wife.[196] Today, the manse is home to *Fables Cottage*, an incredible children's store.

The store, which is located in Ganges, on Hereford Avenue, features books, toys and crafts. The owners are both former Montessori teachers.

Boardwalk Greens

Boardwalk Greens is a charming, outdoor garden shop located in Ganges, at Mouat's Landing.

Salt Spring Island

Stuff & Nonsense

Stuff and Nonsense offers an eclectic mix of fun and practical clothing, linens, dishware, home accessories, books and jewelry. The store is located in Fulford, on Fulford-Ganges Road.

Volume II Island Books

Volume II Island Books is a bookstore that specializes in Gulf Island publications. The store is located in Ganges, at Mouat's Mall.

West of the Moon

West Of The Moon sits on the site of the first post office ever to exist in Ganges. They offer alternative children's toys and activities made by local craftspeople and the finest international toy manufacturers. The store is located in Ganges, beside Mouat's Mall.

Love My Kitchen

Love My Kitchen is a gift store that specializes in kitchen and housewares. It is located in Ganges, in the Harbour Market Building on Fulford-Ganges Road.

Sabine's Bookshop

Sabine's Bookshop offers fine, used and rare books, and feature a large maritime collection. The bookstore is located at Ganges Harbour, in Grace Point Square.

Salt Spring Books

Salt Spring Books carries an eclectic mix of books, magazines, nautical charts, and art cards and supplies. It is located in Ganges, in the Salt Spring Island Trading Company building.

Family Jewels

The *Family Jewels* offers a wide selection of quality jewellery. The store is located in Ganges, on Fulford-Ganges Road.

Galleries to Admire

In the 1850's, when the first group of settlers arrived on Salt Spring Island,[197] a former Black slave from the U.S. proceeded to establish a farm, in what would later become the community of Fernwood.[198] More than one hundred years later, a painter moved with her husband into the farmhouse that had once belonged to his family.[199]

> **Treasure Hunt**
> *A life-sized sculpture of a mermaid sits in a park. Can you find it on Salt Spring?*

Around that time, a group of aspiring artists formed the Salt Spring Painters' Guild.[200] Today, the Guild has about 100 active members.

Along with other artisans, some painters work all winter long, in their homes and studios, to fill the demand of tourists in the summer. During the tourist season, the Guild puts on an annual art show, and holds arts and crafts exhibits around the Island.

Salt Spring is famous for its *Self-Guided Studio Tour*, which allows visitors to see the work of artisans in their private studios from May to September. On Thursdays, visitors can watch them demonstrate their craft.

A Studio Tour map, which is available at the Visitor Information Centre, displays the locations of the 40 participating studios. Look for the white road signs and the chance to meet an artist working in their studio.

There are numerous art galleries located on the Island. On Friday nights, most galleries keep extended hours. If you prefer to participate in a guided tour of Salt Spring's finest art, you can contact Island Gourmet Safaris. They provide for full day tours of the Island's art and studios. Phone: (250) 537-4118

ArtCraft

In the 1960's, the Gulf Islands' Community Arts Council was formed and an annual art show began on Salt

Spring. It featured arts and crafts produced by artists throughout the Gulf Islands. In the year 1980, the art show was moved to a heritage hall.[201]

Today, the art show is called *ArtCraft*. The internationally renowned exhibition is the largest and longest-running art show in all the Gulf Islands. The show represents over 200 local artists and artisans.

ArtCraft is open from May to September. Other, shorter ArtCraft exhibits are held in the spring and during the Christmas season. The exhibit is located in Ganges, at Mahon Memorial Hall, on Lower Ganges Road.

Galleons Lap Photography

In the 1930's, one of the Mouat brothers donated some land for *St. George's Anglican Church*.[202]

Much later, in the 1990's, the church was moved across the street and became *All Saints By The Sea*.[203]

However, the church hall was not moved[204] and, today, it is the home of a gallery, called *Galleons Lap Photography*.

The gallery promotes the work of both contemporary and historic photographic artists. Located in Ganges, on Park Drive, it hosts shows in a broad spectrum of themes.

Stone Walrus Gallery

At the onset of World War I, the first bank on Salt Spring moved into a new building in Ganges.[205] At that time, the building that had originally been its home became the private residence of the manager of the Salt Spring Island Trading Company down the street.[206]

Today, the building is the home of the *Stone Walrus Gallery*. The gallery offers a collection of world art. It is located in Ganges, on Lower Ganges Road.

Salt Spring Island

Meredith Studio Gallery

In the 1980's, a Salt Spring Islander started creating beautiful and functional pottery. Later, a painter starting painting landscapes, seascapes and florals. Recently, the two artists were wed. At that time, they transformed their art studios into the *Meredith Studio Gallery*.[207]

Today, the gallery offers paintings and pottery by these local artists. It is located in Vesuvius, on Vesuvius Bay Road.

Thunderbird Gallery

The *Thunderbird Gallery* features native and local works of art. Sculptures in stone, bronze and wood highlight the collection. The gallery, which also hosts a monthly wine tasting and art show, is located at Ganges Harbour, in Grace Point Square.

Stone Fish Sculpture Studio

The *Stone Fish Sculpture Studio* features creations set in stone. The artist chips, sands, shapes, and then polishes rock into beautiful pieces of art. His work is found in collections throughout the world. The gallery is located in Ganges, on Lower Ganges Road.

Pegasus Gallery Of Canadian Art

In the 1960's, an established art gallery was moved to Salt Spring and became the *Pegasus Gallery of Canadian Art*.[208] Today, the gallery provides for contemporary jewellery, paintings, sculptures, glassware and West Coast aboriginal masks.

The gallery specializes in museum quality antique basketry and work by Northwest Coast native carvers.

It also features paintings by local painter Carol Evans, who is renowned for her limited edition prints and watercolors, as well as by Robert Bateman, who is one of Canada's most well known wildlife artists and environmental activists. The gallery is located in Ganges, at Mouat's Mall.

Morningside Folk Art Studio

The *Morningside Folk Art Studio* offers unique and interesting paper mache sculptures. It is located in Fulford, on Orchard Road.

Frankly Scarlet

Frankly Scarlet is a fine jewelry store that is located at Ganges Harbour, in Grace Point Square.

Jill Louise Campbell Gallery

The *Jill Louise Campbell Gallery* is the largest gallery on Salt Spring. It features impressionist watercolors from the American Southwest, Europe and the Pacific Northwest. The gallery is located in Ganges, at Mouat's Landing.

The Ark

In the late 1880's, the Portuguese storekeeper constructed a small Catholic chapel on Vesuvius Bay. A church bell was hung from the front gable.[209]

The chapel was sold during World War II. At that time, it was converted into a private residence, called *The Ark*.[210]

Today, The Ark is a studio that offers artistic reproductions of dog portraits. The studio is located in Vesuvius, on Vesuvius Bay Road. Unfortunately, the church bell went missing in the 1980's.[211]

Waterfront Gallery

In the 1970's, an office building was constructed in front of the Salt Spring Island Trading Company.[212] It was called the *Ganges Centre Building*.

Soon, a small group of artisans founded an artist's co-operative, and then opened a gallery in the building.[213]

Today, the gallery, which represents over 75 Gulf Islands' artisans, is called the *Waterfront Gallery*. It is located in Ganges, at the Ganges Centre building near Mouat's Mall.

J. Mitchell Gallery

The *J. Mitchell Gallery* features quality artworks crafted from the studios of 38 first-class local artists.

The original works featured in the gallery are created from a variety of mediums, including clay, stone, brass, wood, paper, pottery and fibre. The gallery is located at Ganges Harbour, in Grace Point Square.

Salt Spring Island

Events to Attend

During World War I, Mouat's Trading Company sponsored a Ford Model `T` Car Rally.[214]

The car rally started in Ganges, in front of Mouat's Store, and then ended in Vesuvius. There, the participants enjoyed a picnic.[215]

Mouat`s Ford Car Rally in 1914 - Salt Spring Archives 50571

Today, there are a variety of events on Salt Spring Island to watch or participate in. In addition to numerous festivals and exhibitions, other Island events include parades, tournaments and fairs. There is always something to take in on Salt Spring.

Erotica Festival

Salt Spring Islanders start the year with an erotic art show, called the *Erotica Festival*. The week-long show is put on by ArtCraft and features a number of mature extremes in the performing and visual arts, in celebration of Valentine's Day.

Sensual dances, erotic art exhibitions and fashions shows are generally part of the venue, which takes place in February. The event is held at Mahon Memorial Hall on Lower Ganges Road.

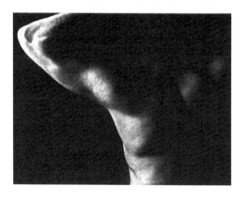

Antique & Classic Car Parade

Although Mouat's Car Rally is long gone, the Salt Spring Antique and Classic Car Club puts on shows and parades throughout the year.

The *Antique and Classic Car Parade* is an annual event that takes place at Easter, in Ganges. Participants frequently dress in clothing from the period, in keeping with the age and style of their car.

Saturday Market in the Park

The infamous *Saturday Market in the Park* began on Salt Spring in the 1970`s. At that time, vendors could sell virtually anything. However, today, market vendors must make, bake or grow their wares themselves.

Over 100 artisans of various types contribute to the Island's international reputation for fine, world-class artists and organic farmers. The market frequently provides for live music, crafts, food and activities. It takes place every Saturday, from April to October, in Centennial Park at Ganges Harbour.

Salt Spring Island

Painters' Guild Art Show

The annual *Salt Spring Painters' Guild Art Show* is a highlight for visitors to the Island. It is a colorful showcase of eclectic paintings produced by Island artists. The event is held in May at ArtSpring.

Round Salt Spring Race

The *Round Salt Spring* sailboat race began on Salt Spring in the 1970's.[216] Today, over 80 boats compete in the 65 km long race, which is hosted by the Salt Spring Island Sailing Club.

The race, which takes place in May, starts and ends in Ganges Harbour. There are prizes for all classes and categories.

Music and Munch

Music and Munch provides for a music festival with an eclectic selection of musical forms. The performances take place every Wednesday, at noon, from June to September. The event is held in Ganges, at the All Saints' Church by the Sea on Park Drive. Lunch is available.

SeaCapers Festival

SeaCapers is a long-lived seaside festival that takes place each year in June. Events are held all around the Island. The festival provides for a parade, biathlon, boat building competition, sand castle building competition and treasure hunt.

Contestants in the Build-a-Boat competition are each given a small sum of money from the local lumberyard to spend on materials. Then, they have just two hours to build a waterproof boat. The winner must demonstrate his craft by paddling it out and back in Ganges Harbour.

Canada Day Celebration

Canada Day Celebrations take place each year on July 1. Food, music and entertainment are provided. There is also a fireworks display.

The main event is held in Centennial Park at Ganges Harbour. Other activities include a concert at ArtSpring and an Antique and Classic Car Show.

Sizzling Summer Nights

The *Sizzling Summer Nights* music festival is a festival of exceptional music. It is held each year at ArtSpring, from July through August.

Festival of the Arts

The *Festival of the Arts* is an annual summer event that has been taking place since the 1980's.[217] The month-long festival provides for a diverse and culturally rich array of talent, which includes performances by local, national and international artists and musicians around the Island. The event takes place throughout the month of July.

Fibre Festival

In the early 1970's, a Salt Spring Islander conceived of the idea of starting weaving classes. She purchased several two-harness table looms, and then persuaded the only known professional weaver on the Island to conduct the classes from her home. When five students enrolled in the classes, the Salt Spring Island Weavers Guild was formed.[218]

The Guild warped late into the night, creating white cotton samplers and a set of four place mats. That summer, they exhibited their works at ArtCraft.[219] Later, in the 1990's, the Guild held their first, annual Sheep-to-Shawl competition. That fall, their works were raffled off at the Fall Fair.[220]

The third competition was held by the Guild at the Farmers Institute. It was called *Fibre Day* and included a Fibre-to-Fabric competition, as well as sheep shearing demonstrations and sheepdog trials. The Guild also held a fun Waulking the Cloth demonstration.[221]

Over the years, as the interest in fine, traditional spinning and weaving grew, Fibre Day evolved into the *Fibre Festival*, a three-day long event that provides for demonstrations and tours of various local fibre arts studios.

The festival celebrates weavers, felt-makers and spinners, as well as craftspeople who use a variety of techniques to make beautiful clothes, wall hangings, rugs and other works of art.

The Fibre Festival takes place in July, at the Farmers Institute on Rainbow Road. It is followed by a fashion show at ArtSpring.

Salt Spring Lavender Festival

The annual *Salt Spring Lavender Festival* is a celebration of lavender, which is held each year, in July. The event is hosted by Sacred Mountain Lavender, the Island's first fully integrated lavender farm. The farm is

Salt Spring Island

located at the south end, on a rocky road, called Musgrave Road.

Treasure Hunt
An Arbutus that is 19` in diameter grows in Mt. Maxwell Park. Can you find it?

Garlic Festival

The annual *Garlic Festival* takes place in August, at the Farmers Institute on Rainbow Road. The event provides for a variety of activities, as well as live music and a lot of food made with a lot of garlic.

Fulford Days

In the early 1920's, the South Salt Spring Island Women's Institute constructed a hall in Fulford. Thereafter, the *Fulford Community Hall* became a venue for several events at the south end, such as fairs, dances, card parties and movies.[222]

Four years after it was built, the furnace was overloaded with paper, causing the chimney to set the roof on fire. The fire destroyed the hall and the Women's Institute was forced to reconstruct it.[223]

In the 1930`s, an arsonist burned the hall to the ground. However, fortunately for the Women's Institute, members of the community rebuilt it.[224]

Salt Spring Island

In the 1940's, the resident who would later build the Akerman Museum purchased 100 pairs of second-hand roller skates. Soon, the neighborhood children were roller-skating in the hall.[225]

Fulford Community Hall in the 1950's - Salt Spring Archives 02186006

Over the years, a lean-to entrance was added to the west end of the hall. It included a balcony where people could watch the roller hockey games.[226]

Today, the hall is host to some of the events that take place during *Fulford Days*, a week-long festival that is held in August.

Fulford Days began in the late 1980's. The main event is held in Drummond Park on Fulford Harbour. It provides for good food, music, competitions and other activities, as well as a fireworks display. A feature of the festival is the pies baked by the Fulford Pie Ladies.

Fulford Hall as it appears today

Salt Spring Island

Garden Faire & Music Festival

The annual *Garden Faire & Music Festival* takes place in August, at Everlasting Summer on McLennan Drive. Live music and activities are provided.

Treasure Hunt
There is a rock displaying a seat from the ship HMS Ganges. Can you find it in a park?

Labour Day Paint-In

During the *Labour Day Paint-In* artists set up their easels around Ganges and demonstrate their painting skills. The event takes place in September.

Salt Spring Fall Fair

After the Mahon Memorial Hall was built in Ganges at the turn of the century, it hosted the *Salt Spring Agricultural Exhibition* for several decades. The exhibitions were so spectacular that they rivaled the famous exhibitions in Vancouver.[227]

The Fall Fair in the 1920`s – Salt Spring Archives 1994137111

Salt Spring Island

Unfortunately, the Salt Spring Exhibition was terminated during World War II. After the war, much smaller exhibitions were held, but those soon ceased, as well.[228]

Much later, in the 1970`s, the Salt Spring Exhibition resumed on the elementary school grounds in Ganges. Three years later, the Farmers Institute purchased its own exhibition grounds nearby and held its first fall fair in the early 1980`s.[229]

Today, the exhibition is called the *Salt Spring Fall Fair*. It provides for a farmer's marketplace and a variety of on-site food vendors. There are riding exhibitions, a midway and live entertainment.

The two-day fair attracts thousands of visitors who attend to see more than 1,500 entries of award-winning displays of produce and livestock. There is judging in a variety of categories, from produce and baking, to sheep shearing and crafts.

As the biggest Island event of the year, the fair takes place in September, at the Farmers Institute hall and fair grounds on Rainbow Road. A shuttle bus is available to transport visitors between Ganges and the fair grounds. The fair is one of the oldest and longest, continuously running fall fairs in all of British Columbia.

Terry Fox Run

In the 1980's, Terrance Fox, a 20-year-old amputee from British Columbia, inspired all Canadians with his 'Marathon of Hope'. His marathon was a run across the country to raise funds for cancer research. The annual *Terry Fox Run* takes place in September.

Salt Spring Island

Street Dance

The *Street Dance* is a festival that is held in August, at Moby's Marine Pub on Upper Ganges Road. Dancers can dance the night away on the streets of Ganges.

Apple Festival

By 1860, **the Postman** had established the Island's first nursery.[230] Named the *Balmoral Nursery*, it produced fruit trees that grew very fast and yielded large fruit. As a result, he was able to meet all the demands for fruit trees from the population of British Columbia in just two years.[231]

The following year, **the Postman** sold his nursery. At that time, it was reported to be the largest nursery in the entire Colony of Vancouver Island.[232]

Later, in the 1890's, the British builder who would later build the Blackburn House planted an orchard of 500 trees on his property, from seeds that his family had gathered while traveling.[233]

Eventually, the builder's family grafted cuttings from over 40 varieties of apples, which had been sent to them from Ireland. To survive the trip, the sender had meticulously embedded each cutting in a potato.[234] Reportedly, one of the varieties of apple trees produced as much as 545 kg of apples.

Wheeling in apples from the orchard, 1920's
Salt Spring Archives 1994137225

Today, Salt Spring Islanders celebrate the apple with an *Apple Festival*, which takes place each year in September, at the Fulford Hall at Fulford Harbour. The event is considered to be the best apple festival in all of North America, offering over 350 varieties of Island-grown apples.

Visitors can participate in an apple tasting event and travel to over one dozen orchards, most of which are organic. For an added treat, they can sample baking by the Fulford Pie Ladies.

Salt Spring Island

Halloween Howl

The *Halloween Howl* is an annual festival that takes place in late October. It features a fireworks display and a haunted house. A masquerade ball is often held at the Beaver Point Hall on Beaver Point Road.

Christmas Celebrations

One winter, during the 1890's, a family's first Christmas on the Island came with a heavy snowfall. To celebrate, they set up a small Christmas tree in their equally small home, and then made decorations out of tiny candles that they clipped onto the tips of the branches.[235]

They made simple, hand-made Christmas gifts for one another and prepared roasts and mincemeat pies for dinner. The steamed plum puddings received a splash of brandy, which they lit on fire. After dinner, they sang carols and roasted chestnuts on the hearth.[236]

Today, Salt Spring Islanders start the Christmas season with a November art show, called the *Wintercraft Festival*. The 10-day sale is put on by ArtCraft and the Guilds of Christmas, and features the works of over 100 artists in 12 different craft guilds. The event is held at Mahon Memorial Hall on Lower Ganges Road.

In December, the Bellingham Central Lions Club, in Washington State, loads the *Christmas Ship* with toys and gifts, and sends it to Salt Spring. Known locally as the *Santa Ship*, the Christmas Ship is greeted in Ganges Harbour, and then Santa and his 'helpers' distribute gifts to the kids.

The season continues with a craft fair, which is held at the south end, at the Beaver Point Hall on Beaver Point Road. The season finishes with carols sung by the Salt Spring Singers.

Polar Bear Swim

The *New Year's Polar Bear Swim* takes place in Vesuvius Bay, on New Year's Day. Hot chocolate is provided to those who brave the cold.

Salt Spring Island Parks & Beaches

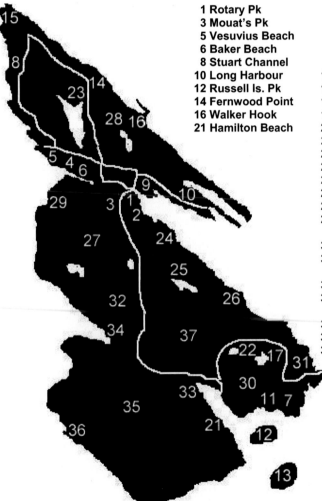

1 Rotary Pk	2 Centennial Pk
3 Mouat's Pk	4 Quarry Drive Pk &
5 Vesuvius Beach	Booth Canal
6 Baker Beach	7 Eleanor Point
8 Stuart Channel	9 Ganges Harbour
10 Long Harbour	11 Seabright Beach
12 Russell Is. Pk	13 Princess Margaret Pk
14 Fernwood Point	15 Arbutus Beach
16 Walker Hook	17 Weston Lake
21 Hamilton Beach	22 Stowell Lake
	23 St. Mary's Lake
	24 Ganges Harbour
	25 Cusheon Lake
	26 Beddis Beach
	27 Manzanita Ridge Pk
	28 Dunbabin Pk
	29 Mount Erskine Pk &
	Bader's Beach
	30 Reginald Hill Pk
	31 Ruckle Pk &
	Beaver Point
	32 Mount Maxwell Pk
	33 Drummond Pk &
	Fulford Harbour
	34 Burgoyne Bay & Pk
	36 Musgrave Point
	37 Andreas Vogt Reserve

Parks to Visit

Before the turn of the century, there was no road to Fulford Harbour - just a narrow trail that led through deep, dark woods. Although the area had been logged, the Douglas-fir and Western Red Cedar trees were gigantic.[237]

The first thing the settlers saw was a ravine, with a creek running through it. The banks of the ravine contained masses of beautiful maidenhair ferns and thousands of wildflowers.[238]

Today, much of Salt Spring Island is parkland. Island Pathways works year-round to establish and maintain a network of pathways and trails. The trails range from short, seashore access, walking trails to forest hikes, so you might want to invest in a pair of *waffle stompers* (hiking shoes).

Salt Spring does not have its own landfill, so a private contractor must transport waste off island. As well as ensuring that nothing is left on the trails, hikers should take as much of their *iktas* (belongings) as possible off the island.

Andreas Vogt Nature Reserve

The *Andreas Vogt Nature Reserve* is located near Fulford. It provides for a forest of Garry Oak and Arbutus trees, as well as views of many of the Island's peaks.

Salt Spring Island

The attractive, 4 km trail through the reserve is of moderate difficulty. It is accessible from the end of a gravel road off Sarah Way. At the gate entrance, the trail to the left crosses a stream bed, and then leads to another trail on the left, which heads to the nature reserve. (#37 on the map)

Burgoyne Bay Provincial Park

Burgoyne Bay Provincial Park is located on the southwest side of the Island. The park, which surrounds a lovely bay, sits in a Douglas-Fir, Garry Oak and Arbutus forest and provides for views of rocky bluffs on Bold Bluff Point.

Numerous trails wander through the historical park with its heritage structures. The trails also provide access to Mount Maxwell to the north and Mount Sullivan to the south. The park is accessible from the end of Burgoyne Bay Road. (#34 on the map)

Centennial Park

In the 1960's, when a boat basin and dock were created in Ganges, the dredging produced enough land for a waterfront park to be created. So the clamshells that were part of the fill were leveled and topsoil was brought in[239] in preparation for the park's development.

The park was named *Centennial Park.* After it was completed, a memorial cenotaph was relocated to the center of the park, from across the street.

Today, Centennial Park is the site of the *Saturday Market in the Park*. The bandstand in the park provides for outdoor entertainment, while the boardwalk offers a wonderful view of Ganges Harbour. There are facilities for picnics if you want to stay a while.

The park provides for a marina, wharf and playgrounds. The wharf is secluded behind a secure breakwater and isolated from the floatplanes and powerboats that pass through the harbour. The park is located at Ganges Harbour, on Fulford-Ganges Road. (#2 on the map)

Drummond Park

In the 1950's, a tall, barefooted, Black resident of Salt Spring made a habit of going down to the beach every morning to see what the tide had brought in.[240]

He would use a broom to sweep the beach. Then, he would put bunches of wild poppies and ferns into soup tins, which he would place in the hollows of old tree trunks.[241]

The Black man treated the beach as his own little 'park' and he loved to invite people from the north end to attend weekend picnics there.[242]

Drummond Park is a recreational park on Fulford Harbour. Established in the early 1970's,[243] it offers playgrounds and a beachfront swimming area. There are also facilities for picnics if you want to stay a while. The park is located on Isabella Point Road. (#33 on the map)

Salt Spring Island

Dunbabin Park

Dunbabin Park is a pristine park on the northeast side of the Island. The easy, 1.5 km trail through the dense, lush park provides for large ferns, Western Red Cedar and Douglas-Fir trees. The trail can be accessed from Stark Road or Robinson Road. (#33 on the map)

Manzanita Ridge Park

Manzanita Ridge Park is a beautiful nature reserve near Ganges. It was acquired only recently, from a long-time Salt Spring Islander.

The park provides for views of neighboring Galiano Island. The strenuous, 3 km trail through the park travels through a forest of 200-year old Douglas-Fir trees. It is accessible from Toynbee Road. (#27 on the map)

> **Treasure Hunt**
> *A Cedar tree that is 26` in diameter grows in Mt. Maxwell Park. Can you find it?*

Mouat Provincial Park

After running Mouat's Store in Ganges for three years, the businesswoman who purchased it converted it into a boarding house. Then, she moved herself, her sons and her store employees into it.[244]

By the onset of World War I, the woman's sons had become successful businessmen. As Mouat Brothers Company Ltd., they acquired the Island's Ford automobile dealership, installed a gas pump at the corner of the store and built a garage across from the boarding house. They also started a taxi service.[245]

Unfortunately, one of the brothers soon contracted polio, which left him paralyzed. Nevertheless, he continued to conduct business from his wheelchair.[246]

Salt Spring Island

Mouat's property holdings in 1912 - Salt Spring Archives 1994137008

In the 1930's, the woman expanded her boarding house, calling it the *Ganges Inn*. It was known locally as *Granny's Boarding House.*[247]

Mouat Provincial Park was named after this family of entrepreneurs, whose company will be celebrating its centennial in the year 2007.[248]

At one time, the park was the Island's only drive-in campground.[249] Today, it provides for a disc golf course. There are also facilities for picnics if you want to stay a while. The forested park provides for beautiful Western Red Cedar trees. It is located in Ganges, on Seaview Avenue. (#3 on the map)

Mt. Erskine Park

Mount Erskine Park is located on the northwest side of the Island. The strenuous 2.5 km trail through the park is called the *Jack Fisher Trail.*

The trail, which travels through Arbutus groves, is accessible from the east side of Collins Road. At the junction, the trail to the right leads to a spectacular viewpoint. (#29 on the map)

Mt. Maxwell Provincial Park

In the early 1860's, an Irishman moved to Salt Spring where he purchased some land in the Fulford-Burgoyne Valley. There, he built a cabin at the foot of a mountain. He was the Island's first legal land owner.[250]

The Irishman started farming with 100 imported, Texas Longhorn cattle. Over time, he became the Island's largest exporter of food, shipping about 20 head of cattle to Vancouver Island each month. Unfortunately, Indian cattle rustlers continuously plagued him.[251]

When the government failed to provide him protection from the Indians, the stubborn Irishman and some other settlers set up an ambush on the mountain range.[252]

When the Indians arrived in their canoes, a white man accompanied them. Upon seeing the Indians, the settlers fired down from the mountain. This panicked the Indians and they fled. Later, they slit the throat of the white man, blaming him for the attack.[253]

Mt. Maxwell in the 1890's
Salt Spring Archives 1994137251

Mount Maxwell was named after this Irishman, whose house was also the home of the post office at Burgoyne Bay.[254]

Mount Maxwell is also known as *Baynes Peak*. The 590 m peak is accessible by way of Mt. Maxwell Road and can be reached by car. The views seen from the mountaintop at sunset are spectacular.

The mountain sits in *Mount Maxwell Provincial Park*, which is located in a secluded area on the west side of the Island. Established in the 1930's, it is the Island's first provincial park.[255]

The old-growth forest park contains the largest Garry Oak, Western Red Cedar,

Arbutus, Western Hemlock and Douglas-Fir trees on the Island. It provides for off-road cycling and there are facilities for picnics if you want to stay a while. The trail through the park is accessible from the end of Seymour Heights Road. (#32 on the map)

Princess Margaret Park Reserve

In the 1870's, an Hawaiian settler came to the Gulf Islands, bringing with him a few other Hawaiians. Soon, they settled on a small Island, which they registered in their names.[256]

The Hawaiian had a unique way of curing tobacco. He would cut a round off a log, bore a hole through the middle, and then fill it with crushed, cured tobacco leaves. Then, he would pour in molasses and rum. When the hole was tightly packed, the log-round would split, producing a long tobacco stick that was ready for smoking.[257]

The Hawaiian's family liked to hold luaus. The parties would begin in his house, and then everyone would travel from home to home. They would remain at each house until they had consumed all the food and drink. Sometimes, the parties would last for weeks.[258]

Around the turn of the century, the Island was sold. The Hawaiian had lived there for over 30 years. When he died two years later, his descendants carried on his unique method of curing tobacco.[259]

Salt Spring Island

Princess Margaret Park is part of the Gulf Islands National Park Reserve. Located on Portland Island, off the southern shore of Salt Spring, it provides for camping and there are facilities for picnics if you want to stay a while. (#13 on the map)

On the network of trails through the park can still be seen the fruit trees, roses and other plants that were grown by the Hawaiians who originally settled there. Bald Eagles and Turkey Vultures are also frequently seen there.

Quarry Drive Park

Quarry Drive Park is located in Vesuvius. The 2 km trail through the park is of moderate difficulty. Accessible from Quarry Drive, it provides for views of Vancouver Island. (#4 on the map)

Reginald Hill Park

Reginald Hill Park is a small public park near Fulford Harbour. The strenuous 1.5 km hike through the park is accessible from the end of Morningside Drive. (#30 on the map)

Reginald Hill, which is located in the park, provides for views of the Fulford-Burgoyne Valley and of Vancouver Island. The breathtaking viewpoint also provides for the only view of the head of Fulford Harbour,

Rotary Marine Park

Rotary Marine Park is located in Ganges, at Mouat's Landing. It provides for a beautiful seaside boardwalk. (#1 on the map)

Recently, the Rotary Club of Salt Spring organized a fundraiser whereby visitors to the park could personalize commemorative paving stones, which were then used to pave the entrance to the park. A local sculptor created the unique, hand-cast stones.

Ruckle Provincial Park

In the 1870's, a settler purchased some land on Beaver Point. There he established a farm. Three years later, he married a woman who had a son from a previous marriage.[260]

> **Treasure Hunt**
> *There is a mural of butterflies painted on the side of a building. Can you find it in Ganges?*

At that time, the settler built a one and one-half storey frame house and the couple started a family of their own. As the family grew, a small addition was added to the house.[261]

In the 1880's, the settler built a wharf, from which he operated the post office at Beaver Point. On his farm, he planted an orchard of 600 trees, establishing a variety of pears, called Ruckle Bartlet.[262] Reportedly, it was the first fruit orchard in all of British Columbia.

The settler also raised dairy Jersey cattle and transported cream to the creamery in Ganges.[263] He grew seed potatoes, which produced as much as 60,000 kg of potatoes each year.[264]

Ruckle farmhouse in the 1890's Salt Spring Archives 992112004

A decade later, two of the settler's sons built homes on his property and brought their brides to live there.[265] At that time, the farm was the largest on the Island.[266]

The settler's adopted son became very adept at woodworking. His magnificent home was fashioned in the Queen Anne style, with handcrafted woodwork and a sharply curved staircase with a gleaming cherry banister.[267]

In the 1930's, the family built yet another home on the property. The house was built for the settler's grandson, who planned to live in it with his bride. Unfortunately, their wedding was cancelled and, thereafter, the house was used to store their potatoes.[268]

Ruckle Provincial Park was named after this family, whose farm is the oldest family farm in all of British Columbia today.[269] The family was granted a life-long tenancy on the property[270] and continues to work the farm.

Ruckle Farmhouse as it appears today

Ruckle Park also provides for off-road cycling and there are facilities for picnics if you want to stay awhile. The park is accessible by way of Beaver Point Road. (#31 on the map)

Russell Island Prov. Marine Park

In the 1870's, an Hawaiian settler emigrated to a tiny island. There, he developed a farm, where he established an orchard and raised sheep and cattle.[272]

At the turn of the century, the Hawaiian died, leaving his entire farm to a young Hawaiian woman. She and her husband built a small frame house on the property and continued to raise sheep and care for the orchard.[273]

The historical park, which was purchased in the 1970's,[271] is located near Fulford Harbour. As the largest park in all the Gulf Islands, it provides for some of the Islands' best hiking through some of the largest Douglas-Fir and Western Red Cedar trees.

Salt Spring Island

Russell Island Provincial Marine Park is located on *Russell Island*, which sits off the southeastern shore of Salt Spring. (#12 on the map)

The park is part of the Gulf Islands National Park Reserve and provides for a forest of Douglas-Fir, Arbutus and Garry Oak. There are stands of Shore Pine that grow around its perimeter.

The frame house that was owned by the Hawaiian immigrant still stands on the Island. The Island is protected by a resident caretaker.

Beaches to Explore

By the year 1858, the English had named the largest of the southern Gulf Islands *Admiral Island*, after a Rear Admiral who was commander in chief of the Pacific Station in Victoria.[274]

When **the Postman** and some other settlers arrived on the Island the following year, they discovered 14 saline springs at the north end, the largest of which was 27 m in diameter. Subsequently, they named that settlement *Salt Spring*.[275]

As more settlers arrived on the Island, they began to refer to the entire Island as *Salt Spring*.[276] So, at the turn of the century, the Geographic Board of Canada conceded to the settlers by officially naming the Island after its springs.[277]

Today, visitors to Salt Spring Island enjoy numerous ocean access beaches. Although there are very few lakes on any of the other Gulf Islands, Salt Spring has 11 lakes, five of which have public beaches. Additionally, It is the only island that contains salt springs.

Arbutus Beach

Southey Point is the most northern tip of the Island. The sandstone beach on the point is called *Arbutus Beach*. The beach is one of the prettiest spots on the Island and provides for views of several nearby islands. Accessible from Arbutus Road, it is a good place to see Sea Stars and a great place for a *soak* (swim).

A second beach access exists at the end of Southey Point Road, which also provides for good swimming. (#15 on the map)

If you launch a boat from the beach, you can travel south, along the shore to Vesuvius. Alternatively, you can travel east to Wallace Island or west around the sandstone formations of Tent and Kuper Islands.

Bader's Beach

Bader's Beach is located on the northwest side of the Island. The wide beach, which is also known as *Erskine Beach* and *Collins Beach*, consists of sand and mud.

At the forest edge of the beach, *Cranberry Creek* provides for a waterfall, which flows down from Mount Erskine and into an outlet, called *Cranberry Outlet*. The beach is accessible from Collins Road. (#29 on the map)

Baker Beach

Booth Bay is located near Vesuvius. The beach on the bay is called *Baker*

Beach. Accessible by way of steps at the end of Baker Road, it is a good place to watch the Bald Eagles soar. (#6 on the map)

Beaver Point

In the 1880's, the British builder and his two sons constructed a one-room schoolhouse on a point. The school was named the *Beaver Point School* and the builder's two sons were the first of the initial 17 students.[278]

During the early 1900's, children from Hawaiian and Indian mixed families made up at least one-half of the enrollment at the school.[279]

In the 1950's, the school closed.[280] When it closed, it held claim to being the oldest continuously running school in all of British Columbia.[281] The little red schoolhouse now operates as a preschool.

Beaver Point is located near Fulford Harbour. There are numerous little coves and bays surrounding the point. The rocky beach, which is located in Ruckle Provincial Park, is accessible by way of trails at the end of Beaver Point Road. (#31 on the map)

Salt Spring Island

Beddis Beach

In the 1880's, the British builder purchased a sailing sloop and loaded it with food, a tent and some household items. Then, he set sail up the west coast with his family.[282] Eventually, the builder and his family landed on a beach, where they constructed a log home.[283]

Later, when the builder contracted pneumonia and died, his sons took over his business.[284] At the turn of the century, they built a new, two-storey, frame house for their family to live in.[285]

Beddis Beach was named after this family of builders,[286] whose home and orchard can still be seen standing nearby.

The stunning white-shell beach is located near Ganges Harbour. It is one of the most beautiful beaches on the Island and provides for views of Prevost Island and Pender Island. A buoy on a rock off the beach commemorates the family who, for many years, left a light burning in the front window of their home, to guide ships through the Pass.[287]

At the north end of the beach is a five-storey cedar and stone structure, called Winsor Castle. It was built from thousands of kilograms of stone, which were hand-picked by an artist, from beaches all over the Gulf Islands.[288]

You can launch a boat from the beach and travel south along the shoreline to the Channel Islands. Alternatively, you can sail to Prevost Island. The beach is accessible from the end of Beddis Road. (#26 on the map)

Booth Canal

In the 1850's, one of the first settlers to arrive on Salt Spring purchased some land surrounding a canal.[289]

About a decade later, the settler became the first representative of Salt Spring in the Legislative Assembly in Victoria.[290]

Salt Spring Island

During his reign as Salt Spring's main politician in the 1870's, letters patent were issued for the incorporation of the Township of Salt Spring Island.[291]

The first meeting saw a number of municipal by-laws passed, which started a battle over the incorporation and divided the Islanders politically for more than a decade.[292]

In the 1880's, the people charged the politician with retaining his political position without election since no one else was nominated to oppose him.[293]

Eventually, the incorporation was cancelled and the politician went on to lose two provincial elections.[294]

In the year 1890, he won again, in a new riding, called 'The Islands'. He held the seat until he passed away. His funeral was the most impressive ever held on Salt Spring.[295]

Booth Canal was named after this politician, whose name also commemorates the adjoining bay. The canal is located near Vesuvius. It provides for a pebbled beach, which is accessible from Quarry Drive, in Quarry Drive Park. (#4 on the map)

Burgoyne Bay

Burgoyne Bay is located in Burgoyne Bay Park, on the southwest side of the Island. It contains significant conservation, recreation, wildlife and fish. Two salmon streams run into the bay and it is a good place to find Sea Stars. At low tide, you can walk along the beach for *lele* (a long time) looking at them.

The rocky beach on the bay provides for a public dock. The trail to the beach is accessible from the end of Burgoyne Bay Road. (#34 on the map)

If you launch a boat from the beach, you can sail north to the Cranberry Outlet or south to Musgrave Landing. However, the bay is exposed to winds from the southeast and northwest.

Cusheon Lake

Cusheon Lake is a warm, freshwater lake near Ganges Harbour. The lake is a very popular swimming area and provides for the Cusheon Creek Fish Hatchery, which is located at the south end of the lake. The lake is accessible from Cusheon Lake Road. (#25 on the map)

Eleanor Point

Eleanor Point is located near Fulford Harbour, in Forest Ridge Park. As the most southeastern tip of the Island, it provides for views of Russell Island. The trail to the point is accessible from the end of Eagles Way. A road to the right leads to the beach on the point. (#7 on the map)

Fernwood Point

Upon landing on Salt Spring in the late 1850's, a few of the first settlers drew straws for their choice of sections of land. As the second settler to choose, the man who would later become **the Postman** chose a parcel of land overlooking a little bay on the northeast side of the Island. On his property, he encountered one of the 14 valuable salt springs.[296]

Within a few months, **the Postman** had built a small log cabin on his valuable property. The cabin had a mud floor and was covered with shakes on poles. It was heated by a small fireplace.

By 1860, he had established the Island's first store and post office. To save postage on his letters, he established a method of writing a message down the page, rotating the paper, and then writing a second message across the first.[297]

In his Balmoral Store, he sold groceries, dry goods and hardware. He would trade with the other settlers for the goods in his store, but would not extend them credit.[298] He would also not allow spitting in his store, nor would he allow swearing if ladies were present. He used a broom to enforce his strict policies.[299]

Over time, the area in which **the Postman** had lived and conducted his business was named in his honor.[300] Today, the area is part of the community known as Fernwood.

Fernwood Point is located in Fernwood. There are three beach accesses on the point, all of which provide for views of Galiano Island.

The access at the end of Fernwood Road leads to a public dock. The dock is surrounded by the only live Sand Dollar beds on the Island.

Two other beach accesses also exist. One access is at the end of Mailview Drive and the other is on North Beach Road. The latter leads to Hudson Point, where the McFadden Creek Heronry is located. (#14 on the map)

If you launch a boat from Hudson Point, you can sail along the shoreline or across to Wallace Island. There is a marine park on the island, which is a great place to see Seals and Bald Eagles.

The protected anchorages in the coves on the west side make it easy to anchor in for the *poolakle* (night). Keep in mind that there are sudden winds in Houstoun Passage.

Fulford Harbour

In the 1860's, the naval ship, HMG *Forward*, was lost in a storm among the Gulf Islands. As the gunboat was being tossed about, the crew suddenly sighted a beacon light. So they pulled into a harbour to ride out the storm.[301]

By the 1890's, a wharf was built in the harbour.[302] It provided a way for a very comfortable passenger vessel, called the *Joan*, to take settlers to and from Vancouver Island.[303]

At that time, most of the area was owned by Hawaiian settlers.[304] However, by the 1920's, a white settlement began to develop around the harbour and a general store, church, community hall and Inn were built nearby. There was even an ice cream kiosk at the wharf.[305]

Around that time, a carpenter built a ferry in the harbour. It was called *Hepburn's Ferry* and was powered by a farm tractor. It could carry four cars to Vancouver Island in two hours.[306]

There were several pulleys on the ferry's drive shaft. So, if the ferry needed more power during the voyage, the owner would just attach a belt from the rear wheel of a car to the ferry's drive shaft, and then start the car.[307]

In the late 1920's, the Gulf Islands Ferry Company was formed. At that time, a ship, which was purchased from the Canadian Pacific Railway, was converted into a ferryboat, called the MV *Cy Peck*. It could carry 20 small automobiles.[308]

Salt Spring Island

Fulford Harbour in the 1920's - Salt Spring Archives 0011179041

Fulford Harbour wharf in the 1930's
Salt Spring Archives 1994137295

In the early 1950's, one of the owners of Mouat's Store purchased the Gulf Islands Ferry Company, and then drastically improved it.[309] The following year, the *Cy Peck* was carrying over 17,000 cars. At that time, it provided the only connection to Vancouver Island.[310]

Fulford Harbour as it appears today

Fulford Harbour is located on the southeast side of the Island. The beach at the head of the harbour was once known locally as *Jackson's Beach*.[311] It sits in Drummond Park and is accessible by way of Isabella Point Road. (#33 on the map)

> **Treasure Hunt**
> *An Indian petroglyph of a seal sits in a park. Can you find it on Salt Spring?*

The wharf in the harbour provides for the busiest ferry terminal on the Island. It still services ferries traveling to and from the tip of Vancouver Island.

Fulford Harbour wharf as it appears today

There are also two public docks in the harbour and a marina that provides for all season overnight moorage.

The community of Fulford is located at the head of the harbour. It is a busy seaside village where businesses and residents co-exist. In addition to the store, church, community hall and Inn, which are all still standing, it offers some delightful galleries, shops and cafes.

Ganges Harbour

In the year 1860, 14 Bella Bella Indians were carrying a load of furs in a canoe.[312] Accompanying them was the renegade white man who would later be killed by Indians following an ambush on Mount Maxwell.[313]

The Indians stopped in a harbour where about 50 Cowichan Indians were already camped. The two tribes were long-time rivals and, as a result, a battle ensued.[314]

During the battle, the white man made his way to the home of a settler who lived nearby. When he told the settler about the battle, the settler went to the harbour to investigate.[315]

At the harbour, the settler discovered that eight Bella Bella Indian men had been killed and the remainder taken prisoner. It was a massacre.[316]

Salt Spring Island

Ganges Harbour in 1912, the post office in the background - Salt Spring Archives 1994137020

Ganges Harbour is located on the northeast side of the Island. First named *Admiralty Bay*,[317] it was the site of what is now known as the 'Massacre of Admiralty Bay'.

The harbour provides for two marinas and two government docks. There is an active Salt Spring Sailing Club, and an outpost station for the Royal Vancouver Yacht Club.

Ganges Harbour as it appears today

Sea Star Point, on the north side of the harbour, provides for a lovely beach with wonderful views of Goat Island and the Chain Islands.

The beach is accessible from the end of Churchill Road. (#9 on the map) A second beach access is located further south, off Price Road. (#24 on the map) If you launch a boat from either beach, you can sail out to the little islands.

Hamilton Beach

In the 1890's, a settler emigrated from England to Canada.[318] Six years later, he moved his large family to Salt Spring, on a tugboat, called the *Alert*.[319]

The tugboat pulled into the harbour, dragging two scows that were loaded with the family's household supplies, some lumber, a cat and a canary.[320]

After negotiating with the highways crew for a public road to be built to their property, the family settled on the waterfront. Unfortunately, the only building on the property was a small, bug-infested, log cabin.[321]

The family soon planted hundreds of fruit and nut trees on their property, and then began to build a large, two-storey house on the beach. They called it *Dromore*.[322]

Unfortunately, the carpenter never fulfilled his obligation and, as a result, the house was never finished. Subsequently, the boys who slept upstairs would awaken on cold mornings to find icicles hanging above their heads.[323]

Hamilton Beach was named after this family, who discovered an Indian burial ground on the *Skull Islands*, at the entrance to the harbour.[324]

SaLt SprINg ISLaNd

Hamilton Beach is located on Fulford Harbour. The wide pebbled beach, which is dotted with driftwood, is home to dozens of swans that feed at the estuary. It is accessible from Isabella Point Road. (#21 on the map)

If you launch a boat from the beach, you can sail around Isabella Point. You can continue around the south end and up to Musgrave Landing. Near Cape Keppel is a marine ecological reserve, which is a good place to see wildlife.

LoNg HarbouR

In the 1940's, the Canadian Pacific Railway provided ferry service to and from the mainland. The ferry docked at Fulford Harbour four days a week. The trip took eight long hours.[325]

In the 1960's, another ferry terminal was built, in Long Harbour,[326] to take over the sailings to the mainland.

Long Harbour sits snugly between Nose Point and Scott Point, just north of Ganges Harbour. There are two accesses to the beautiful beach at the harbour. One access is from Beachside Drive and the other is from Ontario Place. (#10 on the map)

If you launch a boat from the beach, you can travel to the tip of Nose Point. From there, you can continue to Prevost Island, which is part of the Gulf Islands National Park Reserve. It offers some of the most scenic shoreline in all the Gulf Islands. However, be careful of the *skookumchuck* (strong currents) around Nose Point.

MuSgrave PoINt

In the 1870's, four brothers emigrated from England to Salt Spring where they established a large sheep farm in a very secluded area. A decade later, another settler purchased their farm.[327]

Musgrave Point was named after this settler who also purchased the brothers' 350 sheep.[328]

The point is located on the southwest side of the Island. Until the 1920's, it was accessible only by water.[329]

The pebble beach on the point provides for a government wharf. The beach is accessible from the end of a long and rocky road, named Musgrave Road. (#36 on the map)

Seabright Beach

In the 1870's, First Nations was allotted a reserve on a beach between what is now known as Fulford Harbour and Beaver Point.[330] The Indians would set up elaborate camps on the reserve and live there throughout the summers, digging for clams along the shores of the harbour.[331]

The Indians would make holes in the beach, into which they would place kindling. Then, they would light the kindling and throw rocks into the holes.[332] The bonfires and torches they used would light up the shoreline like a city.[333]

When the rocks became hot, the freshly-dug clams were dumped into the holes and covered with mats and bags. When the clamshells opened, they would scoop the partially cooked clams out of their shells and thread them onto long, slender sticks. Each stick was then bent to form a hoop and hung over the fire until the clams browned.[334]

The clamshells the Indians left behind on the beaches produced lime in the soil. Later, when the settlers put in crops of potatoes, the lime caused them to become scaly.[335]

Located near Fulford Harbour, *Seabright Beach* sits beside Salt Spring's only Indian Reserve. The beach provides for some of the loveliest shoreline on the Island. It is accessible from the end of Menhinick Drive. (#11 on the map)

St. Mary Lake

In the 1880's, the woman who would later own and operate Mouat's Store emigrated from Scotland with her husband. Soon, they purchased a farm, which was sitting on a lake on Salt Spring.[336]

The house that stood on the farm was not a desirable one. So, in the 1890's, the woman's husband hired a man to build a new home on the property.[337]

**St. Mary's Lake at the turn of the century
Salt Spring Archives 50550**

Six years later, the woman's husband died, due to poor health, and she was left to raise 11 children on her lakeside farm, alone.[338] Her youngest child was an infant who passed away soon after her father.[339]

With the help of her remaining children, the widow continued to run her farm for a decade. After she moved into her boarding house in Ganges, she rented out the farm. At the end of World War I, it was sold.[340]

St. Mary Lake is the largest freshwater lake in the southern Gulf Islands. The widow's home can still be seen standing on the southwest side of the lake today.

St. Mary's Lake as it appears today

The lake is located near Fernwood. The sandy beach on the lake is accessible from North End Road, at the north end of the lake. It is a great place for a swim. (#23 on the map)

Salt Spring Island

Stowell Lake

Stowell Lake is located near Fulford. Originally named *Fisher's Lake*, it was renamed *Emsley's Lake*[341] before it was named *Stowe Lake*, in honor of an early settler. Frequent misspellings have resulted in its current name.[342]

Stowell Lake is a freshwater lake that provides for good swimming. It can be accessed from Beaver Point Road. (#22 on the map)

Stuart Channel

Stuart Channel is located on the northwest side of the Island. There are two accesses to the beach. One access is just south of West Eagle Road and the other is just south of Sunset Drive. The latter sits on a little bay and provides for views of Idol Island and Tent Island. (#8 on the map)

Vesuvius Beach

The first settlers on Salt Spring were landed on a beach from a Hudson's Bay Company steamer.[343] However, the local Indians were aggressive. So the Black immigrants left the beach and moved further inland. There, they chose their land claims.[344]

In the late 1850's, a Black settler and his family arrived on the Island with several head of cattle. Upon landing on the beach, he immediately sent one of his helpers to the property of **the Postman**, to ask for assistance in transporting his family's belongings.[345]

Salt Spring Island

Suddenly, the Indians landed on the beach in their canoes. They were accompanied by the renegade white man.[346]

When the Black settler pointed his gun at the Indians, they climbed into their canoes and proceeded to leave the beach. Just then, a swarm of canoes appeared in the bay, carrying Indians from another band. This prompted an Indian battle at sea, which culminated in another massacre.[347]

Vesuvius Beach is located in Vesuvius. It is the most popular bathing beach on the Island and is one of the best places to watch the sun set. The pebbled beach is accessible by way of steps at the end of Langley Street. (#5 on the map)

The wharf in Vesuvius Bay provides for a small ferry terminal, which services ferries traveling to and from the east side of Vancouver Island. There is also a public dock in the bay.

The village of Vesuvius provides for a general store, a restaurant, a pub and some quaint shops and studios.

Walker Hook

Walker Hook is a small, privately-owned peninsula that hooks around to create an islet off the northeast side of Salt Spring.

The quaint pebbled beach at Walker Hook is accessible from the end of Grantville Road. (#16 on the map)

Weston Lake

Weston Lake is a freshwater lake near Fulford. It was originally named *Olsen's Lake* and was renamed *Stewart's Lake*[348] before being named in honor of an early settler.[349]

The lake, which is accessible from Beaver Point Road, provides for good swimming. (#17 on the map)

Wildlife to Observe

When the first settlers arrived in the southern Gulf Islands, they found a perfect sanctuary for wildlife. Wild pigs rooted in the marshes, elk stalked the hills and the small black bear foraged among the fruit shrubs. The hunting cry of the gray wolf and the scream of the cougar were frequent sounds.

Salt Spring Island

An early cougar hunter
Salt Spring Archives 989024027

Although there are no large predators in the Gulf Islands today, the wildlife is still very diverse. The Islands are a great place to watch wildlife and are most spectacular in the spring. However, although, many species are commonly seen throughout the year, some are more elusive and it requires a bit of luck to spot them.

Some plant and animal specifies found in the Gulf Islands cannot be found anywhere else in Canada. The rarely seen Sharp-Tailed Snake is known to exist only in the Gulf Islands and on parts of Vancouver Island.

There are some interesting species of wildlife that are rare and endangered. However, only the most commonly seen species of wildlife have been listed here.

Marine Mammals

Marine mammals have adapted characteristics to survive and prosper in environments that are hostile to most land mammals. Some migrate from the southern Gulf Islands to tropical habitats that are suitable for birthing.

Northern migrations begin early in the spring and southern migrations begin in the fall. Many marine mammals can frequently be seen swimming through Active Pass, the waterway between Galiano and Mayne Islands.

The Orca Pass initiative is a citizen-led project whereby both Canada and the United States have agreed to cooperate on the preservation and protection of the Orca Pass International Stewardship Area. This area is a delicate marine mammal and sea-life environment around the southern Gulf Islands.

Harbour Porpoises, or Common Porpoises, are small whales that only grow to 1.8 m in length. They are brown to black in color, with a white underside. They can frequently be seen swimming through Active Pass.

Harbour Seals, also known as Common Seals or Leopard Seals, can grow to 1.8 m in length. They are gray with a unique pattern of fine, dark spots. They have a whiskery nose and bulging eyes. Their hind flippers extend backwards.

There was a Canadian bounty on Harbour Seals for several decades after the turn of the century. However, today, they can be found in quiet, rocky places where they can land during low tide.

Seals are the marine mammals you are most likely to see around the southern Gulf Islands, but they will dive into the water if they are approached too closely.

Orcas, also known as Killer Whales, Black Fish or Grampus, are actually dolphins. They are black with a white chest and sides. They sport a white patch above and behind the eye. They can grow to 9.5 m in length and weigh as much as 10,000 kilograms.

Resident whales are almost exclusively fish eaters. However, transient whales eat harbour seals, sea lion pups, birds, and even porpoises and dolphins if they can catch them.

Salt Spring Island

The coast of British Columbia is well known as the place on *Elehe* (Earth) to watch migrating and resident whales feeding and breaching. At the time of this writing, there were 81 resident whales in the southern Gulf Islands, as well as the San Juan Islands and Washington State. They can frequently be seen swimming through Active Pass, usually in pods of 5-25 animals.

Pacific White-Sided Dolphin are greenish-black with a white belly and grey stripes along their sides. They can grow to a length of 2.5 m. Large groups of dolphin readily approach boats in Active Pass in the spring and fall. Fishermen often refer to them as 'lags'.

Sea Lions can grow to 3 m in length and weigh up to 1,000 kg. They are brown to black in color. Some species were put on the U.S. endangered species list and have since been the object of intense study. Some species are intelligent and adaptable, and are often trained as entertainers at ocean parks and zoos.

Around the southern Gulf Islands, sea lions delight in throwing kelp around and body surfing the waves. They can be seen at the west end of Active Pass, either in the water or hauled up on the rocks.

Otters are reddish-brown to black in color. They are intelligent and very playful, frequently floating and swimming on their backs.

Otters became extinct in British Columbia in the 1920's. In the 1960's, 89 otters were reintroduced from Alaska and have begun to spread again, along the west coast of Vancouver Island.

Sea Life

The ocean environment around the southern Gulf Islands supports a delicate, yet complex web of life. When the tide recedes, the depressions that retain water between the rocks are called *tidal pools*, which are natural aquariums for an abundance of vertebrates and invertebrates. *Siwash loggers* (beachcombers) can see this life when the tide goes out.

For those who want to gather filter-feeding shellfish from around the southern Gulf Islands, a permit is required to dig and quantities are limited.

Clams, or Macoma, can live for 20 years or more. Although the Smooth Washington Clam is the mainstay of the clam business, there are several varieties around the southern Gulf Islands, most of which are white in color.

If you find a clam shell on the beach surface, the clam is no longer living in it. However, finding live *luk'-ut-chee* (clams) is not difficult if you look in mixed mud, rock and sand.

The smallest clams, called *Little-Necks*, can be found just beneath the surface. The larger *Butter Clams*, which can live for 20 years, can be found about 20 cm from the surface. The largest and longest-living clams, called *Horse Clams*, can be found about 30 cm from the surface.

Clams feed, breathe and expel waste through tubes that extend up to the surface of the beach. You can tell if there are clams embedded in a beach if you see water squirting out of the sand. A small shovel or hand rake works well to uncover them.

Crabs are reddish-brown to purple in color. Some species of crab can grow to a width of 23 cm and can live for 6 years.

You need a trap to actually land crabs that are large enough to eat and catching crabs is a secret kept by *island crabbers* (Gulf Islanders who catch crab).

Because they prefer a sand or mud ocean bottom, you can see small specimens in shallow waters. In fact, most of the movement you see in tidal pools are crabs scurrying about.

Cockles look somewhat like clams. They are cream-colored with a grey or brown mottled pattern. They have deeply set ridges, which make them easy to identify.

Cockles can often be found on or near the surface of muddy or sandy beaches. Some species can live for up to 16 years.

Jellyfish are not actually fish. They are a member of the invertebrate family. They feed on small fish and zooplankton that become caught in their tentacles where their stinging cells latch onto them. They are usually found floating near the surface of the water or stranded on the beach.

Limpets have an elliptical shell that rises to a peak. Unlike mussels, clams and oysters, limpets have only one shell half, which is usually greenish brown with cream lines radiating down from the peak. The underside has a brown spot in the center.

Limpets can be found attached to the sides of the rocks along the shoreline on the beach.

Mussels found in the southern Gulf Islands are generally dark blue with hints of brown. They can grow to 20 cm in length. They attach themselves to rocks and to wood, especially to pilings.

To gather *to'-luks* (mussels), just locate a colony and pry them loose. As you gather them, make sure the shells are closed tightly or that they snap shut when you grab them.

Oysters are greyish-white in color. Their shells are wavy and mold to the object they attach themselves to. They can grow to 30 cm in length. The Japanese introduced some of the oysters to the southern Gulf Islands, in the 1920's.

The *klógh-klogh* (oyster) can be found attached to rocks on the beach surface. To gather them, you must pry them loose with a sharp tool. If you harvest a supply of oysters, consider leaving the shells on the beach for new generations of oysters.

Sea Stars, or Starfish, are usually purple in color, but can also be a bright coral color. They can grow to over 36 cm in diameter. The Sea Stars around the southern Gulf Islands are carnivores that feed on mussels and barnacles. They flip their stomach out through their mouth and digest their prey from the inside out.

It is not uncommon to see a Sea Star with a partially regenerated limb. If they lose a limb, they can regenerate it.[350] Some good places to find Sea Stars are at Southey Point and Burgoyne Bay.

Snails have long, cylindrical-shaped shells that are gray to brown in color. The shell often has a stripe winding around it. They only grow to 3 cm, but they can live for 10 years. You can find them in shallow water. The Japanese accidentally introduced some species of snails to the Gulf Islands, in the 1920's.

Land Mammals

Hunting is no longer permitted in the Gulf Islands, except by bow and arrow. Because of that, the land mammals that live there are relatively tame.

Columbia Blacktail Deer, or Mowich, are a small sub-species of mule deer. They are the largest land mammals you are likely to see in the southern Gulf Islands.

A major difference between the Columbian Blacktail and other deer is in the way they can leap, and then land with all four legs hitting the ground at the same time. This enables them to change direction in one bound.

You can identify the seasons by the development of a buck's antlers. In the spring, the buds appear on his head. In summer, he grows lush velvet, which coats the antlers. In the fall, the velvet falls off, hardening the antler bone underneath. In winter, the antlers are cast off.

Unfortunately, as cute as they are, deer eliminate the forest understory in their search for food and are widespread enough to support the outer Gulf Islands' fence builders. You can find them just about everywhere.

Douglas Squirrels, or Chickaree, are brown rodents with a bushy tail and a distinctive call. They make their home in tree cavities or in nests constructed of twigs, needles and bark. You can see them leaping from branch to branch in the dense forests around the southern Gulf Islands.

Raccoons have soft, dense, grey fur and a black mask across their face. They have long tails that are characterized by a pattern of rings. You can see raccoons along some of the beaches around the southern Gulf Islands. Their presence is revealed by human-like handprints, which can be seen in the mud.

Townsend's Chipmunks are brown rodents with black stripes. They

hibernate during the winter months. However, in the summer, because they seldom climb trees, they can be seen scurrying along the ground in the dense forests around the southern Gulf Islands.

Birds

The southern Gulf Islands are well known for their bird watching opportunities. The rocky shores are stopover sites for migratory birds and nesting sites for many sea birds.

Over 130 species of marine birds from 22 countries breed, migrate and/or spend the winter in the Strait. Because the climate invites them to reside or visit, the southern Gulf Islands become a *kalakala* (bird) watchers' paradise in the winter. The south side of Ganges Harbour provides for a protected bird sanctuary on Maple Bay.

Bald Eagles have a white head and tail, and a contrasting brown body. They can grow to 90 cm tall with a wingspan of 2 m.

Although they are indigenous to North America, they were on the brink of extinction late in the 20th century. Fortunately, they have largely recovered and, today, 25 percent of the world's eagle nesting population is found in British Columbia.

Salt Spring Island

Eagles are birds of prey. Their main food supply is the Glaucous-Winged Gull. In the summer, they search for surface-feeding fish, snatching food with aerial acrobatics. They are also good at forcing other birds to drop their prey and will often steal prey from an Osprey.

Eagles are commonly seen around the southern Gulf Islands, especially in the spring when they are rearing their young. Those that are old enough to nest often return to the area in which they were raised. Their nests, which are protected by law, can span 3 m across and weigh 900 kg. They eventually collapse under their own weight.

Because 'Baldies' prefer nest sites with a view, a good place to see them is on Booth Bay and in Princess Margaret Park.

Belted Kingfishers have deep blue or bluish-gray plumage with white markings. The blue feathers on their heads make their heads appear larger than they are. They have a broad, white collar around their neck and a blue band around their chest. The female has an orange band, as well. As loners, they only tolerate one another at mating time.

The Belted Kingfisher is the only species of kingfisher found in the Pacific Northwest. Whenever there is good fishing around the southern Gulf Islands, you can expect to find them perched on trees or posts, close to the water. They are a noisy bird with a loud, rattling call. On a calm winter day, the kingfisher's call can often be heard across a bay.

Brown Creepers have a mottled brown coloration and long, stiff tail-feathers. Their cheerful song has been described as 'trees, trees, trees, see the trees'.

Brown Creepers are common, year-round residents of the forests on the Islands. A creeper will typically forage upwards on tree bark. As it nears the treetop, it drops to the base of a nearby tree to begin its ascent all over again. If it is frightened, it will flatten itself against the tree trunk, becoming almost impossible to see.

Canada Geese have a black head and neck. They have a broad, white chin strap with a contrasting brown body. In flight, they slice through the skies in 'V-formations' or in long lines.

Canada Geese mate for life and are faithful to their breeding grounds, returning to their birth sites each spring. They are abundant waterfowl that can be found year-round.

Cormorants are dark, long-necked, diving birds with long bills. They often stand upright and hold their wings out to dry. They can be seen flying in single file, floating low in the water, or hanging out on rocks or pilings in a bay.

Great Blue Herons, also known as a Shagpoke or Shikspoke, are long-legged, greyish-blue, wading birds. They can grow to 1.2 m tall with a 2 m wingspan. They have a plume of black feathers behind their eye.

Great Blue Herons can be seen standing like sentinels, gazing into the water at low tide, in search of food. They feed in shallow water and spear fish or frogs with their long, sharp bills. They will also raid goldfish ponds in Islanders' backyards. You can hear them croak as they fly laboriously to their enormous nests of sticks.

The herons found in the southern Gulf Islands are a distinctive subspecies. They are year-round residents. Unfortunately, the specific habitat requirements for Herons and their susceptibility to human disturbance pose an increasing threat to the subspecies. As a result, the Canadian Nature Federation designated a 120-

nest heronry, called The McFadden Creek Heronry on Hudson Point, in the 1980`s.

Grouse generally have a brown camouflage pattern. Some species are so well camouflaged that they allow humans, and even predators, to approach very closely. Grouse are year-round, ground-dwelling residents of the Islands' forests. First Nations used to boil them in a soup.

Gulls are graceful in flight, voracious when feeding and capable of many sounds. One small, delicate species is most often seen around the southern Gulf Islands in winter. However, other species can be found, year-round.

Ospreys are mostly white underneath, with contrasting dark coloration above. They display a dark line through their eye. Most Ospreys depart the southern Gulf Islands in the fall and return in the spring.

Ospreys are aggressors and birds of prey. An Osprey will attack an eagle if it comes too close to its nest.

When an Osprey sees a fish in the water, it will suddenly tuck in its wings and plummet down, throwing its feet forward at the last minute. It will then grasp the fish with its talons and carry it with its head forward, to cut down on wind resistance. For this reason, some people refer to them as 'fish hawks'.

Pacific Loons are dark brown with a white belly. In winter, they display a border between the front and the back of their neck. This changes in the summer when they display a velvety grey head, a dark throat and a checkered back.

Loons are diving birds, preferring areas of *skookumchuck* (strong currents), where they dive for fish. Sometimes, in the spring, hundreds of them can be seen diving in Active Pass. In summer, they display a velvety grey head, a dark throat and a checkered back.

In winter, Pacific Loons display a border between the front and the back of their neck. Some of North America's largest wintering population exists in the southern Gulf Islands. They arrive in the fall from their northern breeding grounds.

Red-Breasted Nuthatches are small, short-tailed birds with sharp beaks. They have a black cap with a white eye-stripe and a bit of rusty coloring on their chest. When they are building a nest, their hammering can sound like that of a woodpecker.

Unlike the Brown Creeper, nuthatches spiral down tree trunks, headfirst, pulling insects out of the bark. They will stay close to home year-round if there is enough food or a bird feeder in the area. They can be found in the mature, cone-bearing forests around the southern Gulf Islands, where their call is a familiar sound.

Red-Tailed Hawks have broad wings and a broad, rust-colored tail. They are designed for soaring on thermals of warm, rising air. They are birds of prey and will eat almost any small animal.

The blood-curdling scream of a Red-Tailed Hawk is what is often heard in the movies. They can be found virtually everywhere in the southern Gulf Islands, year-round.

Rufous Hummingbirds can fly left, right, up, down, backwards and even upside down. When hovering, they hold their bodies upright and flap their wings horizontally in a 'figure eight'. Most 'hummers' flap their wings 12,000 times per minute, which is why they are seen as a blur.

Rufous Hummingbirds must eat half their weight in sugar each day. In early spring, they leave their wintering grounds in Mexico and make their way north, flower-by-flower, sucking the nectar from the bloom of the Red-Flowering Currant and Salmonberry shrubs. A long, stiletto bill assists them in this lifestyle. They can be found in the Islands' forests and gardens.

Steller's Jays are the avian emblem of British Columbia. They are deep bluish-black in color and are frequently mistaken for the eastern Blue Jay. They have a dark crest that raises and lowers to indicate their state of agitation.

Announcing their arrival with a raucous call, Steller's Jays will descend upon a bird feeder, scattering smaller birds from it. As year-round residents that live on the Islands' forest slopes, they also like to grab acorns from trees, such as Garry Oak.

Swallows winter in South America and are seen in the southern Gulf Islands in the summer. Several varieties exist, ranging in color from blue to green to brown to purple.

In the last half of the 20th century, the population of Western Purple Martins, the largest species in the swallow family, has declined drastically.

Since the 1980's, the Georgia Basin Ecological Assessment and Restoration Society has helped the population recover by installing more than 1,100 nest boxes throughout the Strait. Young Purple Martins see the nest boxes and return to them each spring.[351]

Turkey Vultures have two-toned wings and a naked, red head. They are birds of prey that are usually seen in flight with wings in a 'V-formation'.

Their tilting flight is an energy-saving strategy. Without turning it's head, a Turkey Vulture can see views of the land below. It will spiral upwards within a thermal of warm, rising air, then descend in a long glide to catch the next thermal.

In the fall, Turkey Vultures use the southern Gulf Islands as stepping stones as they head south to California and Mexico.

Places to Fish

Gulf Island waters are renowned throughout North America for their salmon, bottom fish and shellfish.

Bold Bluff Point is one of the finest salmon-fishing areas in the Gulf Islands.

Salt Spring Island

You can also fish for salmon off Southey Point and at the head of Fulford Harbour.

Active Pass is a prized salmon-fishing ground, providing the best summer fishing in the Gulf Islands and salmon fishing in the Georgia Strait is a year-round sport, with the best fishing occurring in winter.

Active Pass is famous for some of the greatest Spring and Coho salmon fishing in the world. It is a crossroads for salmon returning to spawn in the Fraser River, which has the world's largest, natural, salmon runs.

Keep in mind that the excellent fishing occurs in the Pass during months when the ferry traffic is at its highest, and accidents between ferries and sport fishermen have occurred there.

Porlier Pass, off the north end of Galiano Island, is also known for its salmon fishing. However, tides in Porlier Pass run up to 9 knots and are dangerous to small boats.

Some of the finest salmon fishing in the Gulf Islands is off East Point, on the east side on Saturna Island. It is fished throughout the summer by anglers from both sides of Georgia Strait.

Home to sea-run Cutthroat Trout, Chum and Coho Salmon, Lyall Creek, on Saturna Island, has unusually high numbers of fish for the region and provides for good fishing off the mouth of Lyall Harbour.

You can also fish off the rocks at Bellhouse Provincial Park on Galiano Island and between St. John Point and Conconi Reef on Mayne Island.

If the salmon fishing is slow, try fishing for other bottom fish, such as Ling Cod, Red Snapper, Black Bass and Sole.

South Salt Spring Salmon Charters

South Salt Spring Salmon Charters provides for salmon, cod and halibut fishing around Salt Spring. Experienced guides provide one-half or full day trips. Phone (250) 653-4902

Big Catch Fishing Charters

Big Catch Fishing Charters specialize in sightseeing and salmon fishing. All boats are fully equipped and they provide certified professional guides. Phone: (250) 537-0639

Rope'n & Reel'n Charters

Rope'n & Reel'n Charters provides for fishing and sightseeing tours. Phone: (250) 537-9509

Creatures to Cook

In the gold-mining camps of the late 1800's, an expensive egg omelet, called the *Hangtown Fry*, was prepared for hungry gold miners. It contained fried breaded oysters and bacon.[352]

Today, seafood is incredibly easy to prepare. With a little basic knowledge, you can become an expert in no time at all. The most important thing to remember when cooking seafood is not to overcook it. It is also very important to pay strict attention to the health advisories, as paralytic shellfish poisoning is potentially deadly.

Fish

The freshness and flavor of a fish, such as salmon, cod and sole, can be preserved all day by killing it immediately and keeping it cool. To clean the fish, simply slice it lengthwise and remove the gills, as well as the contents of the carcass. Then, wash the fish before wrapping it in paper.

Early settlers eating a meal, 1930's
Salt Spring Archives 1994137079

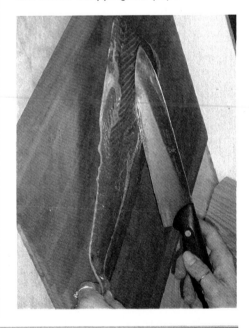

After the fish has been cleaned, cut through the backbone so you can *butterfly it* (spread the two sides down) on a grill or frying pan. Simmer the fish over low heat until the bones can be pulled away from the meat.

Crab

A crab should be kept alive until it is time to cook it. Before you cook a crab, first remove its shell. To remove the shell, point the crab away from your body, and grasp its legs and pinchers with your hands facing up. Hit it against a hard surface so the top of its shell lifts off.

Then, simply break the crab in half and discard the contents of the carcass. To cook the carcass, just boil it and serve it with melted butter for dipping.

Clams and Mussels

To cook clams or mussels, just drop them into a pot of boiling water and leave them until their shells open. Discard the green substance from the shells of the clams. Once they have been removed from their shells, you can fry them in butter, or cook them in a pot with bacon, potatoes and milk.

Oysters

It is best to *shuck* (open) oysters right on the beach and leave the shells there for new generations of oysters. Shucked oysters can then be fried with

Worcestershire sauce or added to a chowder. They can even be eaten raw.

If you prefer to cook your oysters, just throw them on hot coals with the cupped half of the shell up and leave them until their shells open.

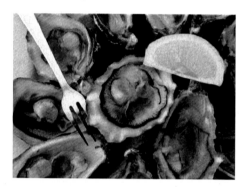

Flora to Appreciate

For most early settlers, timber was an obstruction to destroy, rather than a resource to utilize. When the first settlers began to clear their Island homesteads, they slashed and burned much of the timber they felled.[353]

Many settlers soon supplemented their income by logging, using their horses and oxen to drag logs along skid roads.[354]

At the turn of the century, a building boom boosted the logging industry.

Over the next six years, it grew by over 30 percent, making up 40 percent of British Columbia's economy.[355]

Early settlers falling a tree, 1930's
Salt Spring Archives 1994137078

Today, the unique environment in the Gulf Islands is host to a wide diversity of plant life. The flora is probably the most varied in all of British Columbia.

The southern Gulf Islands sits in one of the smallest climate zones in the west. In this zone, the rain shadow holds rainfall to less than 75 cm annually. The climate zone is noted for over 250 beautiful, spring, wild flowers - too many to list in this little book.

Trees

The southern Gulf Islands are part of the coastal, Douglas-Fir, plant community, which is marked by the predominance of Douglas-Fir, Arbutus and Garry Oak trees. Its very limited range includes only the southern Gulf Islands, Washington State and part of Vancouver Island.

Amabilis means *lovely*. The Amabilis Fir, or Silver Fir, is a tall, straight tree that can grow to 55 m in height. It has flat needles that are dark and shiny, with white lines underneath.

Arbutus, or Madrona, are Canada's only native, broad-leaved evergreen and exist on only a very small portion of the extreme West Coast. They are indigenous to the southern Gulf Islands.

The unusual Arbutus tree produces bright red berries. It sheds its thin, smooth, cinnamon-colored bark. Although they are deciduous, Arbutus do not drop their leaves in the winter.

First Nations believe that the survivors of the *Great Flood* used the Arbutus tree to anchor their canoe to the top of Mount Newton on Vancouver Island.

Today, you can find fine examples of Arbutus in Burgoyne Bay, Mount Maxwell and Mt. Erskine, Russell Island parks, and at the Andreas Vogt Nature Reserve.

Bitter Cherry is a small tree that produces pinkish flowers. The flowers develop into bright red, bitter cherries. First Nations peeled off the stringy bark of the Bitter Cherry for wrapping harpoon and arrow joints.

Black Cottonwood is a hardy tree with a straight trunk. It can grow to 50 m tall. It has large, sticky, fragrant buds. The Black Cottonwood is named for the white hairs on its seeds, which float through the air like wisps of cotton.

First Nations made canoes from cottonwood trees. Some tribes produced soap from the inner bark. The Hudson's Bay Company reportedly continued using this method in their own brand of soaps.

Black Hawthorn is a small tree that produces white flowers. The flowers develop into small, edible, blackish-purple fruits that are shaped like apples. The thorns of the Black Hawthorn were used by First Nations as game pieces when playing games.

Broadleaf Maple, or Bigleaf Maple, is the largest maple tree in Canada, reaching heights of 36 m. Its leaves measure up to 30 cm across. It is restricted to the southwest corner of British Columbia.

First Nations called the Broadleaf Maple the *Paddle Tree* because they made paddles out of the wood.

Cascara is a small tree that produces small, greenish-yellow flowers that develop into bluish-black berries. First Nations boiled the bark of the cascara into a tea that was drank as a strong laxative.

Douglas-Fir, also known as the Oregon Pine or Nootka Pine, is the dominant species of tree in the southern Gulf Islands. It can be found just about everywhere. It can grow to 85 m high and 2 m wide. Its bark is very thick and deeply grooved.

First Nations had many uses for Douglas-Fir. They used it to make fish hooks and handles. They used the wood and boughs as fuel for cooking. Its boughs were frequently used for covering the floors of lodges.

Today, you can find wonderful examples of Douglas-Fir in Mount Maxwell, Burgoyne Bay, Manzanita Ridge, Ruckle, Russell Island and Dunbabin parks.

The Grand Fir is also found in the southern Gulf Islands. It is easily distinguished from other fir trees by its flat needle sprays that grow in two rows.

Garry Oaks, or Oregon White Oaks, are picturesque, gnarled, hardwood trees. They can grow to 20 m in height and can live for up to 500 years. Oaks have thick, grooved, greyish-black bark. They produce small acorns with a scaly cup on one end.

In Canada, Garry Oak are found almost exclusively on the southeastern portion of Vancouver Island, and in the southern Gulf Islands. Unfortunately, their numbers are in decline throughout the range.

Typically, the Garry Oak forms open parkland and meadows. However, from the time the southern Gulf Islands were first settled until the 1950's, much of the land that contained the oak was either logged or converted to farms. Since cone-bearing trees grow faster than

Garry Oak. This creates shade where the oak cannot regenerate.

Although you can find small examples of Garry Oak in the southern Gulf Islands today, less than five percent of the original Garry Oak habitat remains.

Fortunately, Mount Maxwell Park is Canada's largest Garry Oak woodland reserve. It is the best place on the Island to see Garry Oak. Other good places include Burgoyne Bay and Russell Island parks.

Lodgepole Pine trees are commonly cut down for Christmas trees. They can grow to 40 m in height. Their cones often remain closed for years and open from the heat of a fire. This allows them to develop rapidly after a forest fire.

The Western White Pine is also found in the southern Gulf Islands. It is a symmetrical tree that can grow to 40 m in height, or taller. It is a five-needle pine. First Nations called it the *Dancing Tree*. They boiled its bark into a tea, which they drank to treat tuberculosis and rheumatism.

In the early 1900's, a shipment of Eastern White Pine was imported to the mainland from France. It carried a fungus called White Pine Blister Rust, which kills young Western White Pine trees. The fungus spread to the southern Gulf Islands so quickly that, by the 1920's, it was established throughout most of the tree range.[356]

Pacific Crabapple trees produce pinkish, fragrant, apple blossoms. The blossoms develop into small, reddish apples that are somewhat tart. During preservation, the apples become sweeter.

Pacific Dogwood is an irregular tree that produces white flowers with purple tips. The flowers develop into clusters of bright red berries. The blossom of the dogwood is the floral emblem of British Columbia.

Pacific Dogwood is one of the few plants protected by law in British Columbia. However, in spite of its protection, it has often been illegally cut down.

Pacific Willow are tall, slender trees with pale yellow leaves associated with a flower. Although they only grow to 12 m tall, they are one of the largest native willows on the West Coast.

Red Alder is an aggressive, fast-growing hardwood tree that does not live much past 50 years. The wood of the alder provides one of the best fuels for smoking fish.

Sitka Spruce, or Airplane Spruce, are large trees that commonly grow to 70 m tall and 2 m across. First Nations fashioned watertight hats and baskets from the roots, which also provided materials for ropes and fishing line.

Western Hemlock is a large tree that can grow to 50 m tall. It has sweeping branches and feathery foliage. Unfortunately, its shallow rooting system makes it susceptible to being blown over by wind. Because its wood is very easy to work with, some First Nations carved it into dishes.

Mountain Hemlock also grows in the southern Gulf Islands. It has drooping branches that have an upward sweep at the tip. In dense forests, its needles form flat sprays. A good place to find them is in Mount Maxwell Park.

Western Red Cedar, or Canoe Cedar, is British Columbia's official tree. It is very aromatic and has graceful, swooping branches. The cedar can grow to 60 m tall and its trunk spreads widely at its base.

The cedar was considered the *Tree Of Life* by the First Nations who used its wood for dugout canoes, boxes, tools and paddles. From the inner bark, they made rope, clothing, and baskets. Most of their dwellings were constructed of large boards split from cedar logs.

Western Red Cedars live a long life, sometimes to over 1,000 years. As a result, they can be found just about everywhere in the southern Gulf Islands. Some good places to find them is in Mount Maxwell, Ruckle, Mouat and Dunbabin parks.

The Yellow-Cedar is also found in the southern Gulf Islands. It is the oldest tree in the area. Some are 1,500 years old. However, unlike the Western Red Cedar, the crushed leaves of the Yellow-Cedar smell like mildew.

Western Yew, or Pacific Yew, is a small evergreen tree that has reddish, papery bark. Its trunk is often twisted and fluted. Although the yew is a cone-bearing tree, it produces a single seed. A bright red, fleshy cup, which looks like a large berry, surrounds the seed. Beware of the seed, as it is poisonous.

The tough wood of the Western Yew was highly prized by First Nations. Because it displays a polished surface, it was used for carving.

Shrubs and Ferns

A characteristic feature of the shrubs in the southern Gulf Islands is the variety and abundance that exist in the Heather family. These shrubs dominate the understory of the Islands' mature forests, as well as in non-forested habitats. Many of the shrubs give way to edible *olali* (berries). First Nations ate these berries raw or boiled into cakes.

Black Raspberry, or Blackcap, is an erect shrub that has stems with curved prickles. It produces pinkish flowers that develop into hairy, purplish-black berries that are very tasty.

Black Twinberry, or Bearberry Honeysuckle, is an erect to straggly shrub. It produces yellow, tubular flowers, which develop into pairs of shiny, black, inedible berries.

Bog Cranberry is a dwarf shrub that only grows to 40 cm tall. It produces deep pink flowers that have petals that bend backwards. Its berries are pale pink to dark red in color.

Bracken Fern has a stout stem with a feathery frond. Its fronds were used by First Nations as a protective layer in food storage containers, on berry-drying racks and in pit ovens.

Copperbush is a leafy shrub with loose, shredding, copper-colored bark. Its flowers are also copper-colored. Its fruit develop as round capsules. It is one of only a few of the plants in its classification found exclusively in Western North America.

Devil's Club is an erect to sprawling shrub. It has thick, crooked stems that are often entangled and armed with numerous, large, yellowish spines. The wood of the shrub has a sweet smell.

Its leaves are shaped like that of a maple leaf and it produces white flowers.

Related to the Ginseng plant, Devil's Club is one of the most important of all medicinal plants. Sticks made from Devil's Club were used by First Nations as protective charms. When burned, the charcoal from this shrub was used to make face paint for dancers and for tattoo ink.

Dull Oregon Grape is a common, low-growing evergreen shrub with leaves that resemble that of holly. Bright yellow flowers appear in the spring, followed by dark purple, edible berries in the summer. The berries make great jelly. Tall Oregon Grape is another shrub that can be found in the southern Gulf Islands, but in drier areas.

Evergreen Huckleberry has branches that bear leathery leaves lined with sharp teeth. Its clusters of pink flowers produce black berries with a flavor similar to that of a blueberry. Black

Mountain Huckleberry is also found in the southern Gulf Islands. It thrives in old burned sites that have only sparse tree regeneration.

False Azalea, or False Huckleberry, is an erect to straggly, spreading shrub, which resembles both the Azalea plant, as well as huckleberry plants. It produces pink to yellow flowers, which develop into inedible fruit. The leaves turn a bright crimson color in the fall.

False Box is a low, dense, evergreen shrub that resembles the Kinnikinnick plant. It produces tiny, maroon colored flowers that have a pleasant fragrance. It has reddish-brown branches that are often used in floral arrangements.

Goats' Beard, or Spaghetti Flower, is a robust rose bush. It produces white flower clusters that resemble goats' beards. First Nations used the roots for medicinal purposes.

Gummy Gooseberry is an erect to spreading shrub with sticky leaves. It produces reddish colored flowers in drooping clusters. Its flowers, which produce nectar that is eaten by hummingbirds, develop into dark purple, hairy berries. The Wild Gooseberry, which produces green or purple flowers, can also be found in the southern Gulf Islands.

Gorse is a non-native shrub with vicious spines that can form impenetrable thickets. Unlike most plants that grow poorly in soils low in nitrogen, it can remove nitrogen from the air. This enables it to thrive in soils that are low in nitrogen. Gorse is a fire hazard.

Hairy Manzanita is an erect or spreading evergreen with very hairy leaves. Its branches have reddish-brown bark that peels. It produces pinkish flowers in hairy clusters. Manzanita means *little apples*, which describes its edible, coffee colored berries.

Hardhack, or Steeplebush, is an erect, leggy shrub with many woolly branches. It produces rose colored flowers in a long, narrow cluster. Its fruit develop as clusters of numerous, small, pod-like follicles.

Himalayan Blackberry is an immigrant species from India, which was brought to North America in the 1880's. It has sharp, curved spines that make this precursor of barbed wire a plant to be treated with respect. Gulf Islanders pull the deadly branches towards them using a straightened coat hanger.

Himalayan Blackberry produces fine white or pink flowers. The fruit, which is a favorite among berry pickers, is easily mistaken for a raspberry. However, unlike the blackberry, the fruit of the raspberry is hollow when picked.

The Himalayan Blackberry grows in abundance in the southern Gulf Islands.

Indian-Plum, or Osoberry, is a tall shrub with purplish-brown bark. It is one of the first plants to flower in the spring, at which time it produces greenish-white flowers in long clusters. Its flowers, which have an unusual scent, are produced before its leaves appear. Its fruit, which is often referred to as *choke-cherries*, resembles small plums.

Kinnikinnick, or Common Bearberry, is a creeping, evergreen, ground cover that forms dense mats. It has small, pinkish flowers. The flowers produce bright red, berries that resemble miniature apples.

Mock Orange is an erect shrub with peeling bark. It produces broad, white, fragrant flowers that develop into oval, woody fruit. First Nations used the wood for making bows and arrows.

Ocean Spray, also called Creambush or Ironwood, is an erect shrub with peeling bark. It produces creamy flowers in dense clusters that resemble lilacs. The flowers remain on the plant over the winter. The strong wood of the shrub was used by First Nations to make knitting needles and other tools.

Orange Honeysuckle, also called Ghost's Swing or Owl's Swing, is a climbing vine that can reach 6 m in height. It produces long, orange, trumpet-shaped flowers with a sweet nectar deep inside. Because they can reach into the flower to suck its nectar, they are a favorite of hummingbirds.

The fruit of the Orange Honeysuckle develop as bunches of translucent, orange berries. Coastal Indian children also liked to suck the nectar from the base of the honeysuckle flower.

Pacific Ninebark is an erect to spreading shrub with what is believed to be nine layers of peeling bark. It produces small, white flowers that develop into reddish bunches of fruit. First Nations made knitting needles from the wood.

Red Flowering Currant is a tall, erect shrub. It produces white to red flowers in drooping clusters that indicate the beginning of spring. The flowers, which attract hummingbirds, develop into bluish-black berries that are edible, but not very tasty.

Red Elderberry, or Red Elder, is a tall shrub that can grow to 6 m. It produces clusters of creamy flowers with a strong, unpleasant odor. The flowers develop into bright red fruit. Blue Elderberry, which produces blue fruit, can also be found in the southern Gulf Islands.

Red-Osier Dogwood is a spreading shrub that can grow to 6 m tall. The branches are often bright red in color. It produces small clusters of greenish flowers, which develop into bluish-white fruit. Although the fruit is very bitter, dogwood is a very important source of food for the deer in the southern Gulf Islands.

Salal means *this plentiful shrub*. This is for good reason, as it is probably the most dominant shrub in the Islands' forests. Salal is an upright or ground crawling plant that can grow sparsely or form a dense barrier that is almost impossible to penetrate. It spreads by suckering layer upon layer.

Salal produces pink flowers that give way to bluish-black berries. The berries, which are juicy, sweet and aromatic, make excellent jams, jellies and wine.

Salmonberry is a branching shrub that often forms dense thickets. It produces pink, red or purple flowers. The flowers develop into mushy, edible, yellow or salmon colored berries. The berries of the Salmonberry are one of the earliest berries to ripen in the spring.

Scotch Broom is a bushy shrub with long, thin stems from which sprout yellow flowers in the spring and pea-shaped pods in the summer.

In the mid-1800's, a European sea captain was immigrating to Vancouver

Island. He brought with him some Scotch Broom seeds that he had picked up from the Hawaiian Islands. Like Gorse, broom can remove the nitrogen it needs from the air, so when the first white settlers began to arrive, it quickly invaded the southern Gulf Islands.[357]

Today, Scotch Broom grows in abundance in the southern Gulf Islands. It produces a toxin that can depress the heart and nervous system. It is also a fire hazard. Gulf Islanders can often be seen participating in a *Broom Bash* (an event where Broom is destroyed).

Sitka Alder is a tall shrub that can grow to 5 m. It produces a spike-like flower cluster. It also produces clusters of cones from which tiny nuts can be shaken.

Sitka Mountain Ash is an erect shrub that produces small, white clusters of flowers. Its red, berry-like fruits are edible, but very bitter.

Stink Currant is an erect shrub with a skunky smell. It produces greenish clusters of flowers that develop into long clusters of edible, bluish-black berries.

Soopolallie, also called Soapberry or Canadian Buffalo-Berry, is a spreading shrub with branches that are covered with scabs. It produces yellowish-brown flowers. Its bright red berries, which feel soapy to the touch, were used by First Nations to make ice cream.

Sword-Fern, also known as the Pala-Pala plant, is one of the most abundant of the ferns found in the southern Gulf Islands. It is often found growing, along with Western Red Cedar, in damp shady forests. Deer Fern, which resembles the Sword-Fern, also grows in the southern Gulf Islands.

White-Flowered Rhododendron is a slender, erect shrub with peeling bark. It produces clusters of creamy, cup-shaped flowers. Rhododendron is often found along with the False Azalea and Copperbush plants.

Salt Spring Island

Credits

Historical Photos

British Columbia Archives and Records Services

Royal British Columbia Museum

British Columbia Ferry Services Archives

Salt Spring Archives

Galiano Museum & Archives

Management of The Old Farmhouse B&B

Current Photos

Dreamstime™
Tony Campbell, David Coleman, Galina Barskaya, Paul Wolf, Scott Pehrson, Marilyn Barbone, Steffen Foerster, Steve Degenhardt, Melissa King, Randy McKown, Kutt Niinepuu, Dennis Sabo, Jason Cheever, Ryan Tacay, Costin Cojocaru, Marilyna Barbone, Nick Stubbs, Francois etienne Du plessis, Pete Setrac, Penny Riches, Dwight Hegel, Tom Hirtreiter, Elena Ray, Norman Pogson, Hannu Liivaar, Patricia Marroquin, Franc Podgorsek, Keith Naylor, Marilyn Barbone, Jackie Egginton, Vlad Turchenko, Emin Kuliyev, Fred Goldstein, Mehmet Alci

Kevin Oke Photography
Salt Spring Island Fall Fair, Saturday Market in the Park, Portland Island

Georgia Strait Alliance
Orca Pass International Stewardship Area

Gulf Islands Water Taxi
Water Taxis

Harbour Air
Beaver Planes

Everlasting Summer
Everlasting Summer Garden Aerial View

AppleLuscious Organic Orchards
Apple Festival

Graffiti Theatre
Seven Stories Theatrical Production

Gulf Islands Community Arts Council
ArtCraft

The Author

Vicky Lindholm moved with her husband to Mayne Island, in December of 2004. Having authored over 30 pieces of computer courseware, she brought with her more than 20 years of writing experience.

Salt Spring Island: Facts And Folklore is just one in a series of books of its kind to be written by this author. She reviewed over 50 existing pieces of literature and explored parks, beaches and wildlife in order to produce this historical view of Salt Spring Island. The book is an historical guide to the events, landmarks, parks, beaches, shops, restaurants and wildlife on Salt Spring. It includes over 200 photos, past to present, most of which the author and her husband photographed themselves.

Vicky currently lives and works on Mayne Island. In addition to making a living as a writer, she manages a small gift store, as a home-based business, from her residential property.

Notes

[1] **Salt Spring: The Story of an Island** – Charles Kahn, pp. 77

[2] **A Voice from the Past** - The Gulf Islands Guardian, Spring, 1993, pp. 28 & 29

[3] **A Voice from the Past** - The Gulf Islands Guardian, Spring, 1993, pp. 28 & 29

[4] **Salt Spring Island**: Bea Hamilton, pp. 35 and **Salt Spring: The Story of an Island** – Charles Kahn, pp. 42, 46

[5] **Salt Spring: The Story of an Island** – Charles Kahn, pp. 275

[6] **Salt Spring: The Story of an Island** – Charles Kahn, pp. 46

[7] **Homesteads and Snug Harbours: The Gulf Islands** – Peter Murray, pp. 91, 92, 95 & 120

[8] **Homesteads and Snug Harbours: The Gulf Islands** – Peter Murray, pp. 97

[9] **Homesteads and Snug Harbours: The Gulf Islands** – Peter Murray, pp. 97

[10] **Salt Spring: The Story of an Island** – Charles Kahn, pp. 60

[11] **Homesteads and Snug Harbours: The Gulf Islands** – Peter Murray, pp. 91 & 120

[12] **Salt Spring: The Story of an Island** – Charles Kahn, pp. 89, 99 & 101

[13] **Salt Spring: The Story of an Island** – Charles Kahn, pp. 89, 99 & 101

[14] **Homesteads and Snug Harbours: The Gulf Islands** – Peter Murray, pp. 91 & 120

[15] **Salt Spring Island**: Bea Hamilton, pp. 35

[16] **Salt Spring: The Story of an Island** – Charles Kahn, pp. 112

[17] **Salt Spring: The Story of an Island** – Charles Kahn, pp. 37

[18] **Salt Spring: The Story of an Island** – Charles Kahn, pp. 37 & 42

[19] **Salt Spring: The Story of an Island** – Charles Kahn, pp. 41 & 42

[20] **Salt Spring Island: An Illustrated Pamphlet With Map** – Rev. E.F. Wilson, 1894, pp. 26

[21] **Salt Spring Island: An Illustrated Pamphlet With Map** – Rev. E.F. Wilson, 1894, pp. 26

[22] **Salt Spring: The Story of an Island** – Charles Kahn, pp. 174

[23] **St. Mark's On The Hill**: John Rhodes Sturdy, 1965, pp. 12

[24] **Mayne Island & The Outer Gulf Islands**: A History – Marie Elliott, pp. 96

[25] **Homesteads and Snug Harbours: The Gulf Islands** – Peter Murray, pp. 95 & 96

[26] **A Voice from the Past** - The Gulf Islands Guardian, Spring, 1993, pp. 30

[27] **Salt Spring Island**: Bea Hamilton, pp. 39

[28] **A Voice from the Past** - The Gulf Islands Guardian, Spring, 1993, pp. 30

[29] **Homesteads and Snug Harbours: The Gulf Islands** – Peter Murray, pp. 96 & 97

[30] **Salt Spring: The Story of an Island** – Charles Kahn, pp. 54

[31] **The Post Offices of British Columbia**: 1858-1970 - George H. Melvin, pp. 106 and **Salt Spring Island**: Bea Hamilton, pp. 39

[32] **The Post Offices of British Columbia**: 1858-1970 - George H. Melvin, pp. 143 and **Salt Spring: The Story of an Island** – Charles Kahn, pp. 97, 122 & 139

[33] **The Post Offices of British Columbia**: 1858-1970 - George H. Melvin, pp. 143

Notes

[34] **Island Heritage Buildings** – Thomas K. Ovanin, Islands Trust, pp. 60

[35] **Salt Spring: The Story of an Island** – Charles Kahn, pp. 122

[36] **Salt Spring: The Story of an Island** – Charles Kahn, pp. 122

[37] **The Post Offices of British Columbia:** 1858-1970 - George H. Melvin, pp. 106 and **Salt Spring Island:** Bea Hamilton, pp. 40

[38] **The Post Offices of British Columbia:** 1858-1970 - George H. Melvin, pp. 43

[39] **Snapshots of Early Salt Spring and other Favoured Islands:** Mouat's Trading Co. Ltd., pp. 82

[40] **Salt Spring Island:** Bea Hamilton, pp. 89

[41] **Mouat's Landing History Hall**

[42] **The Post Offices of British Columbia:** 1858-1970 - George H. Melvin, pp. 9, 16, 42 & 114

[43] **The Post Offices of British Columbia:** 1858-1970 - George H. Melvin, pp. 42 & 114 and **Salt Spring: The Story of an Island** – Charles Kahn, pp. 143

[44] **The Post Offices of British Columbia:** 1858-1970 - George H. Melvin, pp. 42 & 114 and **Salt Spring: The Story of an Island** – Charles Kahn, pp. 143

[45] **Salt Spring Island:** Bea Hamilton, pp. 88

[46] **The Akerman Family:** Growing Up With Salt Spring Island – Bob Akerman & Linda Sherwood, pp. 166

[47] **Salt Spring: The Story of an Island** – Charles Kahn, pp. 145 & 209

[48] **The Post Offices of British Columbia:** 1858-1970 - George H. Melvin, pp. 76

[49] **The Post Offices of British Columbia:** 1858-1970 - George H. Melvin, pp. 9, 42, 75 & 114

[50] **The Post Offices of British Columbia:** 1858-1970 - George H. Melvin, pp. 42 & 114

[51] **The Post Offices of British Columbia:** 1858-1970 - George H. Melvin, pp. 42 & 114 and **Salt Spring:** The Story of an Island – Charles Kahn, pp. 229 & 267

[52] **The Post Offices of British Columbia:** 1858-1970 - George H. Melvin, pp. 9 & 76

[53] **Salt Spring Island:** An Illustrated Pamphlet With Map – Rev. E.F. Wilson, 1894, pp. 22

[54] **Salt Spring Island:** Bea Hamilton, pp. 23 & 24

[55] **Salt Spring Island:** An Illustrated Pamphlet With Map – Rev. E.F. Wilson, 1894, pp. 22

[56] **Islands Farmers Institute** – Edward Walter, 1902

[57] **Salt Spring: The Story of an Island** – Charles Kahn, pp. 161 & 162

[58] **Salt Spring: The Story of an Island** – Charles Kahn, pp. 237

[59] **Salt Spring: The Story of an Island** – Charles Kahn, pp. 237

[60] **Salt Spring: The Story of an Island** – Charles Kahn, pp. 281

[61] **Salt Spring: The Story of an Island** – Charles Kahn, pp. 236

[62] **Salt Spring Island:** Bea Hamilton, pp. 35 & 173

[63] **Salt Spring: The Story of an Island** – Charles Kahn, pp. 236 & 237

Notes

[64] **Places of Historical Interest in Ganges Village:** A Walking Tour – Salt Spring Historical Society

[65] **Salt Spring:** The Story of an Island – Charles Kahn, pp. 122 & 123

[66] **Mary Hawkins Memorial Library website**

[67] **Salt Spring:** The Story of an Island – Charles Kahn, pp. 272

[68] **Mary Hawkins Memorial Library website**

[69] **Mary Hawkins Memorial Library website**

[70] **Salt Spring:** The Story of an Island – Charles Kahn, pp. 272

[71] **Salt Spring:** The Story of an Island – Charles Kahn, pp. 144 & 145

[72] **Salt Spring:** The Story of an Island – Charles Kahn, pp. 144 & 145

[73] **Salt Spring:** The Story of an Island – Charles Kahn, pp. 144-146 & 148

[74] **Salt Spring:** The Story of an Island – Charles Kahn, pp. 144-146 & 148

[75] **Snapshots of Early Salt Spring and other Favoured Islands:** Mouat's Trading Co. Ltd., pp. 79

[76] **Snapshots of Early Salt Spring and other Favoured Islands:** Mouat's Trading Co. Ltd., pp. 51

[77] **Salt Spring:** The Story of an Island – Charles Kahn, pp. 150

[78] **Mouat's Trading Company website**

[79] **Mouat's Trading Company website**

[80] **Mouat's Trading Company website**

[81] **Salt Spring:** The Story of an Island – Charles Kahn, pp. 185

[82] **Island Heritage Buildings** – Thomas K. Ovanin, Islands Trust, pp. 69

[83] **Island Heritage Buildings** – Thomas K. Ovanin, Islands Trust, pp. 69

[84] **Southern Gulf Islands:** An Altitude SuperGuide – Spalding, Montgomery and Pitt, pp. 114

[85] **Island Heritage Buildings** – Thomas K. Ovanin, Islands Trust, pp. 69

[86] **Salt Spring:** The Story of an Island – Charles Kahn, pp. 246

[87] **Salt Spring:** The Story of an Island – Charles Kahn, pp. 270 & 297

[88] **Salt Spring:** The Story of an Island – Charles Kahn, pp. 270 & 297

[89] **Salt Spring:** The Story of an Island – Charles Kahn, pp. 297

[90] **Salt Spring:** The Story of an Island – Charles Kahn, pp. 84

[91] **Mayne Island & The Outer Gulf Islands:** A History – Marie Elliott, pp. 24

[92] **Salt Spring Island:** An Illustrated Pamphlet With Map – Rev. E.F. Wilson, 1894, pp. 24

[93] **Salt Spring:** The Story of an Island – Charles Kahn, pp. 84

[94] **Salt Spring Island:** An Illustrated Pamphlet With Map – Rev. E.F. Wilson, 1894, pp. 24

[95] **Salt Spring:** The Story of an Island – Charles Kahn, pp. 163

[96] **Salt Spring:** The Story of an Island – Charles Kahn, pp. 162

[97] **Salt Spring:** The Story of an Island – Charles Kahn, pp. 162

Notes

[98] **Salt Spring Island:** Bea Hamilton, pp. 156

[99] **Salt Spring Island:** Bea Hamilton, pp. 156

[100] **Salt Spring:** The Story of an Island – Charles Kahn, pp. 235

[101] **Salt Spring Island:** Bea Hamilton, pp. 156

[102] **Island Heritage Buildings** – Thomas K. Ovanin, Islands Trust, pp. 71

[103] **Island Heritage Buildings** – Thomas K. Ovanin, Islands Trust, pp. 71

[104] **Salt Spring:** The Story of an Island – Charles Kahn, pp. 288

[105] **Salt Spring:** The Story of an Island – Charles Kahn, pp. 289

[106] **Snapshots of Early Salt Spring and other Favoured Islands:** Mouat's Trading Co. Ltd., pp. 44

[107] **Salt Spring:** The Story of an Island – Charles Kahn, pp. 150

[108] **Island Heritage Buildings** – Thomas K. Ovanin, Islands Trust, pp. 63

[109] **Island Heritage Buildings** – Thomas K. Ovanin, Islands Trust, pp. 63

[110] **Island Heritage Buildings** – Thomas K. Ovanin, Islands Trust, pp. 63

[111] **Island Heritage Buildings** – Thomas K. Ovanin, Islands Trust, pp. 63

[112] **Salt Spring:** The Story of an Island – Charles Kahn, pp. 265

[113] **Salt Spring:** The Story of an Island – Charles Kahn, pp. 130 & 131

[114] **Salt Spring:** The Story of an Island – Charles Kahn, pp. 150

[115] **Salt Spring:** The Story of an Island – Charles Kahn, pp. 150

[116] **Salt Spring:** The Story of an Island – Charles Kahn, pp. 225

[117] **Salt Spring:** The Story of an Island – Charles Kahn, pp. 225

[118] **Salt Spring:** The Story of an Island – Charles Kahn, pp. 225

[119] **Salt Spring:** The Story of an Island – Charles Kahn, pp. 224

[120] **Salt Spring:** The Story of an Island – Charles Kahn, pp. 297

[121] **Salt Spring:** The Story of an Island – Charles Kahn, pp. 131

[122] **Salt Spring Archives website**

[123] **Conversations with Hastings House Country Estate staff**

[124] **Southern Gulf Islands**: An Altitude SuperGuide – Spalding, Montgomery and Pitt, pp. 117

[125] **Fulford Creek Guest House website**

[126] **Fulford Creek Guest House website**

[127] **Island Heritage Buildings** – Thomas K. Ovanin, Islands Trust, pp. 60

[128] **Island Heritage Buildings** – Thomas K. Ovanin, Islands Trust, pp. 60

[129] **Island Heritage Buildings** – Thomas K. Ovanin, Islands Trust, pp. 60

[130] **Snapshots of Early Salt Spring and other Favoured Islands:** Mouat's Trading Co. Ltd., pp. 44

[131] **Salt Spring Island:** Bea Hamilton, pp. 72

[132] **Salt Spring Island:** Bea Hamilton, pp. 72

[133] **Snapshots of Early Salt Spring and other Favoured Islands:** Mouat's Trading Co. Ltd., pp. 44 and **Salt Spring:** The Story of an Island – Charles Kahn, pp. 145 & 209

Notes

[134] **Snapshots of Early Salt Spring and other Favoured Islands:** Mouat's Trading Co. Ltd., pp. 44 and **Salt Spring:** The Story of an Island – Charles Kahn, pp. 145 & 209

[135] **The Post Offices of British Columbia:** 1858-1970 - George H. Melvin, pp. 118

[136] **Snapshots of Early Salt Spring and other Favoured Islands:** Mouat's Trading Co. Ltd., pp. 44

[137] **Salt Spring Island:** Bea Hamilton, pp. 60

[138] **The Heritage of Salt Spring Island:** a Map of Treasures – Island Pathways

[139] **Salt Spring:** The Story of an Island – Charles Kahn, pp. 108 & 111

[140] **Island Heritage Buildings** – Thomas K. Ovanin, Islands Trust, pp. 82

[141] **Island Heritage Buildings** – Thomas K. Ovanin, Islands Trust, pp. 82

[142] **Island Heritage Buildings** – Thomas K. Ovanin, Islands Trust, pp. 60

[143] **Island Heritage Buildings** – Thomas K. Ovanin, Islands Trust, pp. 60

[144] **Salt Spring Island Archives website**

[145] **Island Heritage Buildings** – Thomas K. Ovanin, Islands Trust, pp. 60

[146] **Island Heritage Buildings** – Thomas K. Ovanin, Islands Trust, pp. 78

[147] **Island Heritage Buildings** – Thomas K. Ovanin, Islands Trust, pp. 78 and **Salt Spring:** The Story of an Island – Charles Kahn, pp. 113 & 120

[148] **Salt Spring Island:** Bea Hamilton, pp. 169 and **Salt Spring:** The Story of an Island – Charles Kahn, pp. 113 & 120

[149] **Island Heritage Buildings** – Thomas K. Ovanin, Islands Trust, pp. 78

[150] **Island Heritage Buildings** – Thomas K. Ovanin, Islands Trust, pp. 78

[151] **Salt Spring Island:** A Place To Be – Ellie Thorburn and Pearl Gray, pp. 30

[152] **Island Heritage Buildings** – Thomas K. Ovanin, Islands Trust, pp. 49

[153] **Island Heritage Buildings** – Thomas K. Ovanin, Islands Trust, pp. 49

[154] **Salt Spring:** The Story of an Island – Charles Kahn, pp. 181

[155] **Salt Spring Island:** A Place To Be – Ellie Thorburn and Pearl Gray, pp. 63

[156] **Island Heritage Buildings** – Thomas K. Ovanin, Islands Trust, pp. 49

[157] **Salt Spring:** The Story of an Island – Charles Kahn, pp. 312

[158] **Salt Spring Island:** Bea Hamilton, pp. 118 and **Salt Spring:** The Story of an Island – Charles Kahn, pp. 133 & 134

[159] **Snapshots of Early Salt Spring and other Favoured Islands:** Mouat's Trading Co. Ltd., pp. 106 and **Salt Spring Island:** A Place To Be – Ellie Thorburn and Pearl Gray, pp. 146

[160] **Island Heritage Buildings** – Thomas K. Ovanin, Islands Trust, pp. 75

[161] **Island Heritage Buildings** – Thomas K. Ovanin, Islands Trust, pp. 75 and **Salt Spring:** The Story of an Island – Charles Kahn, pp. 158

[162] **Island Heritage Buildings** – Thomas K. Ovanin, Islands Trust, pp. 75 and **Salt Spring:** The Story of an Island – Charles Kahn, pp. 158

[163] **Island Heritage Buildings** – Thomas K. Ovanin, Islands Trust, pp. 75

[164] **Salt Spring:** The Story of an Island – Charles Kahn, pp. 115

Notes

[165] **Salt Spring Island:** Bea Hamilton, pp. 169 and **Salt Spring:** The Story of an Island – Charles Kahn, pp. 115

[166] **Salt Spring Archives website**

[167] **Everlasting Summer website**

[168] **St. Mark's On The Hill:** John Rhodes Sturdy, 1965, pp. 12 and **The Gulf Islanders:** Sound Heritage, Volume V, Number 4, pp. 17

[169] **St. Mark's On The Hill:** John Rhodes Sturdy, 1965, pp. 12 and **The Gulf Islanders:** Sound Heritage, Volume V, Number 4, pp. 17

[170] **The Gulf Islanders:** Sound Heritage, Volume V, Number 4, pp. 17 & 18

[171] **Places of Historical Interest in Ganges Village:** A Walking Tour – Salt Spring Historical Society

[172] **Places of Historical Interest in Ganges Village:** A Walking Tour – Salt Spring Historical Society

[173] **Salt Spring:** The Story of an Island – Charles Kahn, pp. 239

[174] **Salt Spring:** The Story of an Island – Charles Kahn, pp. 239

[175] **Salt Spring:** The Story of an Island – Charles Kahn, pp. 239

[176] **Salt Spring:** The Story of an Island – Charles Kahn, pp. 265

[177] **Salt Spring:** The Story of an Island – Charles Kahn, pp. 225

[178] **Island Heritage Buildings** – Thomas K. Ovanin, Islands Trust, pp. 69

[179] **The Heritage of Salt Spring Island:** a Map of Treasures – Island Pathways

[180] **Salt Spring:** The Story of an Island – Charles Kahn, pp. 176

[181] **Mouat's Trading Company website**

[182] **Mouat's Trading Company website**

[183] **Places of Historical Interest in Ganges Village:** A Walking Tour – Salt Spring Historical Society

[184] **Island Heritage Buildings** – Thomas K. Ovanin, Islands Trust, pp. 69

[185] **The Heritage of Salt Spring Island:** a Map of Treasures – Island Pathways

[186] **Salt Spring:** The Story of an Island – Charles Kahn, pp. 144

[187] **Snapshots of Early Salt Spring and other Favoured Islands:** Mouat's Trading Co. Ltd., pp. 78

[188] **Southern Gulf Islands:** An Altitude SuperGuide – Spalding, Montgomery and Pitt, pp. 116

[189] **Salt Spring:** The Story of an Island – Charles Kahn, pp. 163

[190] **Salt Spring:** The Story of an Island – Charles Kahn, pp. 163

[191] **The Heritage of Salt Spring Island:** a Map of Treasures – Island Pathways

[192] **Salt Spring:** The Story of an Island – Charles Kahn, pp. 280

[193] **Royal Canadian Legion Branch 92 website**

[194] **Royal Canadian Legion Branch 92 website**

[195] **The Heritage of Salt Spring Island:** a Map of Treasures – Island Pathways

[196] **Salt Spring:** The Story of an Island – Charles Kahn, pp. 238 & 239

Notes

[197] **Homesteads and Snug Harbours:** The Gulf Islands – Peter Murray, pp. 91, 92, 95 & 120

[198] **Salt Spring:** The Story of an Island – Charles Kahn, pp. 59

[199] **Salt Spring Island:** A Place To Be – Ellie Thorburn and Pearl Gray, pp. 98

[200] **Salt Spring Island Painters' Guild website**

[201] **Salt Spring Island:** A Place To Be – Ellie Thorburn and Pearl Gray, pp. 59

[202] **Salt Spring:** The Story of an Island – Charles Kahn, pp. 239

[203] **Salt Spring:** The Story of an Island – Charles Kahn, pp. 301

[204] **Places of Historical Interest in Ganges Village:** A Walking Tour – Salt Spring Historical Society

[205] **The Heritage of Salt Spring Island:** a Map of Treasures – Island Pathways

[206] **Places of Historical Interest in Ganges Village:** A Walking Tour – Salt Spring Historical Society

[207] **The Meredith Studio Gallery brochure**

[208] **Discussions with the management of the Pegasus Gallery of Canadian Art**

[209] **Island Heritage Buildings** – Thomas K. Ovanin, Islands Trust, pp. 60 and **Salt Spring:** The Story of an Island – Charles Kahn, pp. 37, 97 & 152

[210] **Island Heritage Buildings** – Thomas K. Ovanin, Islands Trust, pp. 60 and **Salt Spring:** The Story of an Island – Charles Kahn, pp. 37, 97 & 152

[211] **Island Heritage Buildings** – Thomas K. Ovanin, Islands Trust, pp. 86 and **Conversations with the management of The Ark studio gallery**

[212] **Salt Spring:** The Story of an Island – Charles Kahn, pp. 289

[213] **Gulf Islands Online website**

[214] **Salt Spring Archives**

[215] **Salt Spring Archives**

[216] **Salt Spring Island Sailing Club website**

[217] **Salt Spring:** The Story of an Island – Charles Kahn, pp. 310

[218] **Salt Spring Island Weavers & Spinners Guild website**

[219] **Salt Spring Island Weavers & Spinners Guild website**

[220] **Salt Spring Island Weavers & Spinners Guild website**

[221] **Salt Spring Island Weavers & Spinners Guild website**

[222] **Salt Spring:** The Story of an Island – Charles Kahn, pp. 231 & 242

[223] **Salt Spring:** The Story of an Island – Charles Kahn, pp. 231

[224] **Salt Spring:** The Story of an Island – Charles Kahn, pp. 231

[225] **The Akerman Family:** Growing Up With Salt Spring Island – Bob Akerman & Linda Sherwood, pp. 278

[226] **The Akerman Family:** Growing Up With Salt Spring Island – Bob Akerman & Linda Sherwood, pp. 279

[227] **Salt Spring Island:** Bea Hamilton, pp. 110

[228] **Salt Spring:** The Story of an Island – Charles Kahn, pp. 182

Notes

[229] **Salt Spring: The Story of an Island** – Charles Kahn, pp. 182

[230] **Salt Spring: The Story of an Island** – Charles Kahn, pp. 54 & 180

[231] **Letter From Jonathan Begg, of Balmoral Nursery** – November, 1862

[232] **Salt Spring: The Story of an Island** – Charles Kahn, pp. 54

[233] **Salt Spring: The Story of an Island** – Charles Kahn, pp. 119

[234] **Salt Spring: The Story of an Island** – Charles Kahn, pp. 119

[235] **Salt Spring Island:** Bea Hamilton, pp. 130 & 131

[236] **Salt Spring Island:** Bea Hamilton, pp. 130 & 131

[237] **The Gulf Islanders:** Sound Heritage, Volume V, Number 4, pp. 7 & 8

[238] **The Gulf Islanders:** Sound Heritage, Volume V, Number 4, pp. 7 & 8

[239] **Salt Spring: The Story of an Island** – Charles Kahn, pp. 296

[240] **Salt Spring Island:** Bea Hamilton, pp. 172 & 173

[241] **The Akerman Family:** Growing Up With Salt Spring Island – Bob Akerman & Linda Sherwood, pp. 272 and **Salt Spring Island:** Bea Hamilton, pp. 172 & 173

[242] **Salt Spring Island:** Bea Hamilton, pp. 172 & 173

[243] **Salt Spring: The Story of an Island** – Charles Kahn, pp. 296

[244] **Salt Spring: The Story of an Island** – Charles Kahn, pp. 150

[245] **Salt Spring: The Story of an Island** – Charles Kahn, pp. 160

[246] **Salt Spring Island:** Bea Hamilton, pp. 157

[247] **Salt Spring: The Story of an Island** – Charles Kahn, pp. 148

[248] **Mouat's Trading Company website**

[249] **Salt Spring: The Story of an Island** – Charles Kahn, pp. 295

[250] **Salt Spring Island:** Bea Hamilton, pp. 51 & 52 and **Salt Spring: The Story of an Island** – Charles Kahn, pp. 54

[251] **Salt Spring Island:** Bea Hamilton, pp. 51 & 52 and **Salt Spring: The Story of an Island** – Charles Kahn, pp. 54

[252] **Salt Spring Island:** Bea Hamilton, pp. 51 & 52

[253] **Salt Spring Island:** Bea Hamilton, pp. 51 & 52

[254] **Homesteads and Snug Harbours:** The Gulf Islands – Peter Murray, pp. 100 & 101

[255] **Salt Spring: The Story of an Island** – Charles Kahn, pp. 242

[256] **Salt Spring Island:** Bea Hamilton, pp. 79 and **Salt Spring: The Story of an Island** – Charles Kahn, pp. 103

[257] **Salt Spring Island:** Bea Hamilton, pp. 82

[258] **Salt Spring Island:** Bea Hamilton, pp. 83

[259] **Salt Spring Island:** Bea Hamilton, pp. 79 & 82 and **Salt Spring: The Story of an Island** – Charles Kahn, pp. 103

[260] **Island Heritage Buildings** – Thomas K. Ovanin, Islands Trust, pp. 86

[261] **Island Heritage Buildings** – Thomas K. Ovanin, Islands Trust, pp. 86

[262] **Island Heritage Buildings** – Thomas K. Ovanin, Islands Trust, pp. 86

[263] **Island Heritage Buildings** – Thomas K. Ovanin, Islands Trust, pp. 86

Notes

[264] **Times Past:** Salt Spring Island Houses and History Before the Turn of the Century – Community Arts Council Heritage House Committee, pp. 39

[265] **Island Heritage Buildings** – Thomas K. Ovanin, Islands Trust, pp. 86-89

[266] **Salt Spring:** The Story of an Island – Charles Kahn, pp. 94

[267] **Island Heritage Buildings** – Thomas K. Ovanin, Islands Trust, pp. 88

[268] **Island Heritage Buildings** – Thomas K. Ovanin, Islands Trust, pp. 86-89

[269] **Salt Spring:** The Story of an Island – Charles Kahn, pp. 94

[270] **Island Heritage Buildings** – Thomas K. Ovanin, Islands Trust, pp. 86-89

[271] **Salt Spring:** The Story of an Island – Charles Kahn, pp. 94

[272] **Salt Spring:** The Story of an Island – Charles Kahn, pp. 101

[273] **Salt Spring:** The Story of an Island – Charles Kahn, pp. 107

[274] **Salt Spring:** The Story of an Island – Charles Kahn, pp. 11

[275] **A Voice from the Past** - The Gulf Islands Guardian, Spring, 1993, map and **Salt Spring:** The Story of an Island – Charles Kahn, pp. 11

[276] **Salt Spring Island:** An Illustrated Pamphlet With Map – Rev. E.F. Wilson, 1894, pp. 4

[277] **Salt Spring:** The Story of an Island – Charles Kahn, pp. 11

[278] **Gulf Islands Driftwood:** July 21, 1982, pp. 24

[279] **Salt Spring Archives website**

[280] **Salt Spring:** The Story of an Island – Charles Kahn, pp. 237

[281] **Gulf Islands Driftwood:** July 21, 1982, pp. 24

[282] **Salt Spring:** The Story of an Island – Charles Kahn, pp. 118 & 119

[283] **Salt Spring:** The Story of an Island – Charles Kahn, pp. 118 & 119

[284] **Homesteads and Snug Harbours:** The Gulf Islands – Peter Murray, pp. 105

[285] **Island Heritage Buildings** – Thomas K. Ovanin, Islands Trust, pp. 73

[286] **Salt Spring:** The Story of an Island – Charles Kahn, pp. 118 & 119

[287] **Salt Spring Island:** Bea Hamilton, pp. 98

[288] **Salt Spring Island:** Bea Hamilton, pp. 161

[289] **Salt Spring:** The Story of an Island – Charles Kahn, pp. 87

[290] **Homesteads and Snug Harbours:** The Gulf Islands – Peter Murray, pp. 95 & 106

[291] **Homesteads and Snug Harbours:** The Gulf Islands – Peter Murray, pp. 106 & 107

[292] **Homesteads and Snug Harbours:** The Gulf Islands – Peter Murray, pp. 106 & 107

[293] **Salt Spring Island:** Bea Hamilton, pp. 75 & 76

[294] **Homesteads and Snug Harbours:** The Gulf Islands – Peter Murray, pp. 111 and **Salt Spring:** The Story of an Island – Charles Kahn, pp. 87

[295] **Homesteads and Snug Harbours:** The Gulf Islands – Peter Murray, pp. 111 and **Salt Spring:** The Story of an Island – Charles Kahn, pp. 87

[296] **A Voice from the Past** - The Gulf Islands Guardian, Spring, 1993, pp. 29 & 30

[297] **Salt Spring:** The Story of an Island – Charles Kahn, pp. 36

[298] **Homesteads and Snug Harbours:** The Gulf Islands – Peter Murray, pp. 96

Notes

[299] **Salt Spring Island:** Bea Hamilton, pp. 35

[300] **Homesteads and Snug Harbours:** The Gulf Islands – Peter Murray, pp. 96 & 97

[301] **Salt Spring Island:** Bea Hamilton, pp. 68

[302] **Salt Spring Island:** An Illustrated Pamphlet With Map – Rev. E.F. Wilson, 1894, pp. 26

[303] **Salt Spring:** The Story of an Island – Charles Kahn, pp. 139

[304] **Salt Spring Island:** Bea Hamilton, pp. 129

[305] **Salt Spring:** The Story of an Island – Charles Kahn, pp. 229

[306] **The Akerman Family:** Growing Up With Salt Spring Island – Bob Akerman & Linda Sherwood, pp. 166

[307] **The Akerman Family:** Growing Up With Salt Spring Island – Bob Akerman & Linda Sherwood, pp. 166

[308] **Salt Spring:** The Story of an Island – Charles Kahn, pp. 226

[309] **Salt Spring Island:** Bea Hamilton, pp. 157 & 158

[310] **Salt Spring:** The Story of an Island – Charles Kahn, pp. 267 & 268

[311] **The Akerman Family:** Growing Up With Salt Spring Island – Bob Akerman & Linda Sherwood, pp. 272 and **Salt Spring Island:** Bea Hamilton, pp. 172 & 173

[312] **Homesteads and Snug Harbours:** The Gulf Islands – Peter Murray, pp. 93 & 94

[313] **Salt Spring Island:** Bea Hamilton, pp. 51 & 52

[314] **Homesteads and Snug Harbours:** The Gulf Islands – Peter Murray, pp. 93 & 94

[315] **Homesteads and Snug Harbours:** The Gulf Islands – Peter Murray, pp. 93 & 94

[316] **Homesteads and Snug Harbours:** The Gulf Islands – Peter Murray, pp. 93 & 94

[317] **Salt Spring:** The Story of an Island – Charles Kahn, pp. 11

[318] **The Gulf Islanders:** Sound Heritage, Volume V, Number 4, pp. 7 & 8

[319] **Salt Spring Island:** Bea Hamilton, pp. 126

[320] **Salt Spring Island:** Bea Hamilton, pp. 126

[321] **Salt Spring Island:** Bea Hamilton, pp. 129

[322] **Salt Spring Island:** Bea Hamilton, pp. 132

[323] **Salt Spring Island:** Bea Hamilton, pp. 132 & 133

[324] **Salt Spring Island:** Bea Hamilton, pp. 129

[325] **Salt Spring:** The Story of an Island – Charles Kahn, pp. 267, 268 & 277

[326] **Salt Spring:** The Story of an Island – Charles Kahn, pp. 267, 268 & 277

[327] **Salt Spring:** The Story of an Island – Charles Kahn, pp. 95

[328] **Salt Spring:** The Story of an Island – Charles Kahn, pp. 95

[329] **Salt Spring:** The Story of an Island – Charles Kahn, pp. 95 & 230

[330] **The Heritage of Salt Spring Island:** a Map of Treasures – Island Pathways

[331] **Gulf Islanders:** Sound Heritage, Volume V, Number 4, pp. 8

[332] **Salt Spring Island:** An Illustrated Pamphlet With Map – Rev. E.F. Wilson, 1894, pp. 21

[333] **Gulf Islanders:** Sound Heritage, Volume V, Number 4, pp. 8 & 9

Notes

[334] **Salt Spring Island:** An Illustrated Pamphlet With Map – Rev. E.F. Wilson, 1894, pp. 21

[335] **Gulf Islanders:** Sound Heritage, Volume V, Number 4, pp. 8 & 9

[336] **Salt Spring:** The Story of an Island – Charles Kahn, pp. 125 & 126

[337] **Mouat's Trading Company website**

[338] **Salt Spring:** The Story of an Island – Charles Kahn, pp. 125 & 126

[339] **Mouat's Trading Company website**

[340] **Times Past:** Salt Spring Island Houses and History Before the Turn of the Century – Community Arts Council Heritage House Committee, pp. 25

[341] **Salt Spring:** The Story of an Island – Charles Kahn, pp. 13

[342] **The Heritage of Salt Spring Island:** a Map of Treasures – Island Pathways

[343] **Salt Spring Island:** Bea Hamilton, pp. 10

[344] **Salt Spring Island:** Bea Hamilton, pp. 12 & 13

[345] **Salt Spring Island:** Bea Hamilton, pp. 13-16

[346] **Salt Spring Island:** Bea Hamilton, pp. 13-16, 51 & 52

[347] **Salt Spring Island:** Bea Hamilton, pp. 17 & 18

[348] **Salt Spring:** The Story of an Island – Charles Kahn, pp. 13

[349] **The Heritage of Salt Spring Island:** a Map of Treasures – Island Pathways

[350] **Southern Gulf Islands:** An Altitude SuperGuide – Spalding, Montgomery and Pitt, pp. 96

[351] **MayneLiner Magazine:** Volume 15, Number 8, pp. 20

[352] **City of Placerville, California website**

[353] **Salt Spring:** The Story of an Island – Charles Kahn, pp. 201

[354] **Salt Spring:** The Story of an Island – Charles Kahn, pp. 201

[355] **Salt Spring:** The Story of an Island – Charles Kahn, pp. 201

[356] **Plants of the Pacific Northwest Coast:** Washington, Oregon, British Columbia and Alaska

[357] **Plants of the Pacific Northwest Coast:** Washington, Oregon, British Columbia and Alaska

INdeX

INdeX

INdeX

INdeX

INdeX

INdeX

INdeX

INdeX

INdeX